240

Critical Guides to French Texts

Critical Guides to French Texts

EDITED BY ROGER LITTLE, WOLFGANG VAN EMDEN, DAVID WILLIAMS

Beroul's 'Tristan' and the 'Folie de Berne'

Peter S. Noble

Senior Lecturer in French Studies
University of Reading

Grant & Cutler Ltd
1982

© Grant & Cutler Ltd
1982
ISBN 0 7293 0128 1

I.S.B.N. 84-499-5642-0

DEPÓSITO LEGAL: V. 1.370 - 1982

Printed in Spain by
Artes Gráficas Soler, S.A., Valencia
for
GRANT & CUTLER LTD
11 BUCKINGHAM STREET, LONDON W.C.2

Contents

To Margaret

Preface

The *Tristan* by Beroul and the *Folie de Berne* are two of the great poems of Medieval French literature and have both been edited more than once. I have used editions which are most likely to be available to the student, and so all references and quotations are from the edition of Beroul by Professor Ewert (Bibliography, *1*), and to the text of *Folie de Berne* given by Monsieur J.-C. Payen (Bibliography, *53*). It seemed pointless to use the Hoepffner edition of the *Folie* as it is so difficult to obtain.

It is a pleasure to express my thanks to Professor van Emden, who made many helpful suggestions to improve this book, to Dr David Shirt, who gave me invaluable assistance with the bibliography, and to my wife, who not only read and improved the whole book but also gave me the time to write it. The responsibility for the remaining imperfections is mine.

1. Introduction

It has become a cliché to say that very little is known about Beroul but it is none the less true. He gives his own name twice in the fragment, once asserting that he knows the story better than his rivals:

> Berox l'a mex en sen memoire (1268)[1]

once to refer to his source which may or may not have existed:

> Ne, si conme l'estoire dit,
> L[a] ou Berox le vit escrit (1789-90)

Nothing else is known about him for certain. The incomplete text of his poem is preserved in one manuscript, MS fr. 2171 (formerly G. Reg. 7987, Baluze 759) of the Bibliothèque Nationale in Paris. It lacks the beginning and the end, and it is uncertain how much is missing. The manuscript belongs to the second half of the thirteenth century and so is of no help with dating Beroul. In fact, like almost everything else about Beroul, his dates are a source of lively dispute, with dates proposed ranging between 1160 and the early thirteenth century. The evidence for these conflicting theories varies considerably. Dominica Legge has suggested that Beroul may have written his poem for the wedding of Conan of Brittany and Margaret of Scotland, which would explain some of the Scottish references to be found in the text (see 27). This early date has been supported by Tony Hunt, who detects the influence of Abelard's school of philosophy on Beroul's outlook, which would favour an early date, such as the 1160s, when the effects of Abelard's teaching were still important (see 22, especially p.503).

On the other hand, a much later date would have to be accepted if the reading of line 3849 is accepted: 'Les mains gourdes por le mal d'Acre,/les piez enflez por le poacre' (3849-50). This would seem to be a reference to the illnesses suffered during the siege, which took place during 1190 and

[1]All references are to *1* Vol. 1.

1191, and would therefore mean that the poem was written after 1190. There are, however, two problems about this line. It could be an interpolation, in which case its value for dating the poem is nil. Secondly the manuscript actually reads 'le mal dagres' and 'd'Acre' is the emendation of the previous editor Muret, which was accepted by Ewert (see *1*, vol. II, pp.34-36). This reading has been vigorously attacked by Gweneth Whitteridge (see *49*), and certainly a disputed reading is very uncertain evidence for dating a poem. There is the further problem that this reading comes late in the surviving fragment, whose unity is the subject of another fierce dispute.

There is no need to examine the now rejected theories of a multiplicity of authors, but there is still a lively debate whether the surviving fragment is the work of one or two authors. There is not complete unanimity amongst the supporters of the two-author theory about the exact point of the join, which could be as late as 2133 or as early as 1774. The arguments for two authors cite as evidence the apparent contradictions within the poem over the number of enemies conspiring against the lovers, the confusion over who killed the forester, linguistic and technical differences between the two parts of the poem and an apparent change in tone between the first part of the poem and the second, where the court of King Arthur is introduced. Supporters of the one-author theory argue that the contradictions can either be explained or may be the result of episodic composition, that the linguistic and technical difficulties either do not exist or are not significant, and that the change of tone simply reflects the change of scene in the poem, as the characters and the spirit of the poem remain much the same.[2] Some of these points will be discussed in greater detail later in the book, but for the purposes of this study Beroul will be regarded as one author, responsible for the whole poem, contradictions and all, as there is a unity of characterisation and inspiration which convinces me that this poem is the work of one author.

[2]See the sharp exchanges in *39* and *40* with *21* for detailed study of the language. See also *35*, *36* and *37* for a rather less acrimonious debate with *20*.

The linguistic problem is further complicated by discussion over the exact dialect which Beroul used. Although most critics seem to agree that he wrote in Norman, the earlier view that he was from eastern Normandy has been challenged by those who would place him further west and perhaps a little south near the Anjou border, or by others who see him as coming from west Normandy, perhaps from one of the regions conquered from the Bretons, which could mean that he was a French-speaking Breton working for the Normans. This argument is still unresolved and is not helped by the uncertainty about where and for whom he was writing. Clearly Beroul is very familiar with Cornwall, less so with other parts of England, although he has some notion of southern Scotland. E.M.R. Ditmas has shown that all the places mentioned by Beroul are connected with the great Marcher Lords of England, in particular with the families of the Earls of Cornwall and Gloucester, and this has led her to suggest, in contradiction to Legge, that the poem was written for a wedding of a member of this great family.[3] This would also place it later than Legge proposed. Beroul's total lack of interest in south-eastern England does indicate that he had little to do with the royal court. The probabilities are that Beroul came from Normandy, had visited Cornwall and may well have worked for one of its great families.

If the author and his text pose many problems, some of which will probably never be solved, so, of course, does the Tristan legend itself. Ever since Gertrude Schoepperle's great book on the sources of the Tristan legend, in which she argued the case for the material coming from Celtic literature, showing in particular the parallels between the Tristan legend and the Irish saga of Diarmaid and Grainne,[4] scholars have been adding to the evidence in support of such a theory. Evidence from Welsh

[3]Paper delivered by Miss E.M.R. Ditmas at the York meeting of the British Branch of the International Arthurian Society in 1977. See also the recent article by Oliver Padel, The Cornish Background of the Tristan Stories, *Cambridge Medieval Celtic Studies*, 1 (1981) 55-81.

[4]See *43*. S. Eisner, *The Tristan Legend* (Evanston: Northwestern University Press, 1969) sees the Irish legends as collaterals to a Northern British source ultimately derived from Greek legends. This theory does not change the Celtic nature of the immediate source of the Tristan material.

literature reveals the existence of Drystan, son of Tallwch, swineherd to March and lover of Essylt. The framework of the legend seems to have existed therefore in eighth-century Wales. The Celtic background cannot be denied, as the setting itself must indicate. Cornwall and Ireland were still Celtic countries and in Beroul the other countries mentioned are Wales and south-west Scotland (Galloway), also Celtic. The names, including Arthur, are Celtic, the setting is Celtic and much of the material is undoubtedly drawn from Celtic myth or perhaps, if the distinction has to be made, folklore. There can be few who would argue for a purely classical source now, although the influence of classical legends such as the Theseus story on the Tristan legend as a whole cannot be denied. This influence is less obvious in Beroul because we lack the episodes in which it is shown, as in the annual tribute of children paid by Cornwall to Ireland until Tristan's victory over the Morholt brings it to an end, or in the episode of the white and black sails as Tristan waits for the news of Iseut's arrival to cure him of his deadly wound. We do, however, have the episode of the horse's ears, which belongs to Breton folklore as well as to Ovid, an author well known in the Middle Ages.

Recently the possibility of an Oriental source has been energetically supported. The clearest and most concise case for the influence of Oriental literature has been put by Lucie Polak, who has shown the parallels between the Tristan legend and the great Persian tale of Vis and Rahmin. She has also suggested that the Arabian tale of Kais and Lobna could have influenced the Tristan legend too, and it is certain that the parallels are striking (see *34*). The main problem lies in how such material travelled to the West, as the surviving translations of *Vis and Rahmin* postdate Beroul's Tristan. We do, of course, have evidence that the Tristan legend was well known in France before the composition of any of the surviving versions. The troubadours writing in the first half of the twelfth century are aware of the beauty of Iseut and the nobility of Tristan and use them for comparisons. A famous Welsh minstrel, Blehri, is known to have been at the court of Poitou, a centre of culture where Arabs from Spain, Spaniards and southern and northern French, and it seems Celts, could meet. It has been suggested that this may have been the route by which some knowledge of Eastern legends penetrated the West (ibid.). This is not proven, however, although it remains an attractive theory. The possibility of Oriental influence must be added to the certainty of a Celtic base influenced by Latin and ultimately Greek literature, coming together in episodes such as the horse's ears, where Beroul could have drawn on classical and folklore sources.

In spite of all these problems, and there are others not yet mentioned, the poem remains a thrilling and a fascinating one for the reader who is prepared to make an adjustment to the mentality of a different period. Beroul is on one level more accessible than some of his sophisticated contemporaries, because he is less influenced by the difficult doctrine of courtly love. It can be said with certainty that in the second part of the twelfth century there was great interest in the theory of love and that eventually this interest resulted in the production of codes of love, perhaps meant satirically, such as the *De Amore* of Andreas Capellanus, whose ideas on love and marriage undoubtedly differed greatly from twelfth century practice. Beroul shows little interest in the theory of love. Unlike other figures in twelfth century romances his characters do not indulge in introspective self-analysis, which can quickly pall for the modern reader. Instead we are shown the lovers in conflict with their society, and a rough, brutal society it is, perhaps closer to the real twelfth century than the society depicted in either romance or epic. The love interest in Beroul's poem causes it to be classified as a romance but in many ways it resembles two other medieval genres which are usually thought of as being completely separate. The suggestion of group strife — the lovers and their (few) supporters against the evil barons — is very reminiscent of the situation in an epic, where it is almost always a question of the group, be it nation or clan against a rival group, and the quarrel can be settled only by violence. Beroul also shows traces of the outlook of the *fabliaux*, the coarse, earthy poems which flourished in the thirteenth century, although it seems likely that they were in circulation earlier. The broad farce of certain scenes such as the scene at the ford where Tristan tricks his enemies into the mud seems to be related to the cruel humour of the *fabliaux*, where there is little pity for the loser.

The energy and the cruelty of these genres do not conflict with the love interest in Beroul, because the Tristan legend is about the effect of an irresistible love on two beings who thereafter will do anything to satisfy their love. They are aware that they have other responsibilities and duties, but Beroul shows that these cannot compete with their love for one another, and indeed, while the potion lasts, they are careless of anything else at all. In the fragment of Beroul which survives, the author accepts the love without question. As already stated, he does not seek to analyse or to question it, for he is above all a poet of action, and analysis or introspection would slow down his narrative.

The old division of the *Tristans* into 'version commune' and 'version courtoise' is now regarded as too simplistic, but as already indicated, Beroul was not greatly concerned with the nature of the love or with its effects on the characters of the lovers, which would have been the mainstay of a courtly romance. As I hope to show, his version is not without its own sophistication, but it was probably written for an audience who would listen to it and who would need to have their attention held once it had been captured. As a result Beroul cannot afford to allow the pace to drag or the tension to slacken. This may well be the explanation for the apparently episodic method of composition, for it is easy to divide the fragment into different episodes, as done for example by Daniel Poirion (1-572; 573-1305; 1306-1350; 1351-1430; 1431-1636; 1637-1773; 1774-2132; 2133-3027; 3028-4266; 4267-4485),[5] and these episodes can be subdivided into manageable lengths for oral delivery. The very uneven length of the proposed episodes is a problem for this theory, although it is not insurmountable, and there can be no dispute that Beroul's poem does divide easily

[5]See *33*, p.200.

into sections such as those proposed above.

Although Beroul's version of the legend is one of the oldest which survives, it is certain that he was drawing on existing material. He himself refers in line 1267 to the *estoire* and in 1265 to the *contor* who do not know it properly, unlike Beroul himself. Medieval authors, of course, attached great importance to citing sources to prove their own scholarship, even (or especially) when they were being original, but there is no reason to reject Beroul's attack on his rivals, which shows that other versions were in circulation, especially when we also have poems such as the two *Folie Tristan* and the *Lai de Chevrefeuille* of Marie de France which treat episodes which are not found in the surviving fragment of Beroul. Whether the *estoire* is one single work to which all subsequent versions owe their material is another question, however. It seems more likely that there was in circulation a considerable number of shorter poems which were sung by minstrels and which dealt with different episodes in the careers of Tristan and Iseut. These were amalgamating so that before Beroul there may well have been a longer or several longer poems giving a more complete history of the lovers, but there was probably no one definitive version, as Beroul's own comment seems to suggest.

Despite its popularity with critics today, Beroul's version seems to have been the less successful of the two French versions of the second half of the twelfth century. The Anglo-Norman writer Thomas produced a version more influenced by courtly love than that of Beroul, and most of the other surviving versions such as the *Tristan* of Gottfried von Strassburg, the *Norse Saga* and the vast *Prose Tristan* drew their material from the version of Thomas, which despite its great influence also survives only in fragments, although from more manuscripts. The only version close to Beroul is that of the German Eilhart von Oberg, who was clearly drawing on the same material as Beroul, although the two authors diverge increasingly in the last third of the surviving fragment of Beroul. It seems likely that the *Prose Tristan*, which survives in many manuscripts, was so popular that the poems of Beroul and Thomas seemed old-fashioned and difficult to read, so that there was no incentive to preserve them. Tastes have changed, however, and now it is the crisper poems which are preferred, which concentrate on the Tristan material and do not attempt to link it to the vast Arthurian corpus to any great extent, unlike the prose writers of the next century.

2. *The Lovers*

One of Beroul's great strengths as an author is ability to depict character, not so much by outright description, of which there is very little in the text, but through his skill in making the characters come to life by their speech and their actions. Inevitably he is particularly concerned with the lovers, whose story after all this is and with whom he clearly sympathises. The portrayal of Iseut brings vividly to the audience this clever, forceful woman made ruthless by the demands of her love.

From the moment the fragment opens we learn something of her mettle:

> Que nul senblant de rien en face.
>
> Com ele aprisme son ami,
>
> Oiez com el l'a devanci (2-4)

Iseut coming to a forbidden rendez-vous with Tristan has seen the shadow of her husband Mark in the fountain and realises that she is walking into a trap. Her reaction is immediate. She seizes the initiative and will not let Tristan speak until she thinks that he too has realised the danger, which he had already perceived. Her skill with words and the quickness of her mind are such that she is able to devise immediately a formula which means one thing to herself and to Tristan and another to Mark who is listening in the tree:

> Li rois pense que par folie,
>
> Sire Tristran, vos aie amé;
>
> Mais Dex plevis ma loiauté,
>
> Qui sor mon cors mete flaele,
>
> S'onques fors cil qui m'ot pucele
>
> Out m'amistié encor nul jor! (20-25)

Implicitly she denies that there was anything wrong in her affection for Tristan, by contrasting the King's thoughts in the first two lines quoted with the pledge which is to follow. The use of the subjunctive in line 21 cleverly draws attention to the idea

that any evil is in the King's mind. The strongly worded pledge
of her innocence follows, which avoids naming names. The King
believes that he is the man who had her virginity and so is
satisfied, but Iseut and Tristan know that Tristan loved her first
and so she is speaking the truth to him and to God. She goes on
to strengthen this impression of her honesty and her sense of
honour:

> Ne je, par Deu omnipotent,
> N'ai corage de drüerie
> Qui tort a nule vilanie.
> Mex voudroie que je fuse arse,
> Aval le vent la poudre esparse,
> Jor que je vive que amor
> Aie o home qu'o mon seignor. (32-38)

'Seignor' is ambiguous. Tristan knows that she means him, but
Mark naturally interprets 'seignor' as applying to him, her
lawful husband. The whole impression of innocence is carefully
prepared by the use of words like 'drüerie' and 'vilanie', which
she violently rejects. The strength of her oath in line 35 is ironic
in view of the fate which Mark will try to inflict on her when he
discovers that she has been deceiving him. For the moment,
however, it serves to increase the impression of indignation and
innocence which Iseut is creating for the benefit of Mark in the
tree above.

Her whole speech is designed to convince Mark that she is a
dutiful but frightened wife who has answered a call for help
from Tristan because he is Mark's relative. Her fear stems from
her knowledge of Mark and is not feigned, but she can use her
real emotion to serve her own ends, by planting the suggestion
that the trouble is being caused by her enemies at court. Skilfully
she reminds Mark of his debt to Tristan, a theme already
mentioned (27-28):

> Molt vos estut mal endurer
> De la plaie que vos preïstes
> En la batalle que feïstes
> O mon oncle [...] (50-53)

Quite naturally she makes Mark recall that Tristan, alone

amongst his knights, was prepared to defend him against the Morholt. Her friendship with Tristan has an easy explanation:

> [...] Je vos gari;
> Se vos m'en erïez ami,
> N'ert pas mervelle, par ma foi! (53-55)

Tristan owes her a deep debt of gratitude for curing him. Only their enemies could interpret this evilly and they have planted the suspicion in the King's mind:

> Et il ont fait entendre au roi
> Que vos m'amez d'amor vilaine. (56-7)

The denial is all the more effective because it is implied. She warns Tristan that she dare not come again (62-63), because she is so afraid of the King:

> Trop demor ci, n'en quier mentir;
> S'or en savoit li rois un mot,
> Mon cors seret desmenbré tot,
> Et si seroit a molt grant tort;
> Bien sai qu'il me dorroit la mort. (64-68)

Her tactics are changing. At first she was concerned to impress on the King the innocence of her love for Tristan and to remind him of the debt which he owes Tristan. Now she is stressing her fear of death at Mark's hands, but line 67 makes her point that she would be killed wrongfully. Her affection for Tristan is based on her mother's advice to cherish the relations of her husband:

> Je quidai jadis que ma mere
> Amast molt les parenz mon pere,
> Et disoit ce que la mollier
> Nen avroit ja [son] seignor chier
> Qui les parenz n'en amereit;
> Certes, bien sai que voir diset. (73-78)

Tristan's brief interjection (81-84) about untruthful gossip gives her the chance to return to the idea that Mark is a good man led astray by others:

> Molt est cortois li rois, mi sire;
> Ja nu pensast nul jor par lui
> Q'en cest pensé fuson andui;

> Mais l'en puet home desveier,
> Faire le mal et bien laisier;
> Si a l'on fait de mon seignor. (86-91)

'Cortois' flatters Mark, and the use of 'sire' may unconsciously recall the use of 'seignor' in the opening lines and further reassure him that he was the man intended. Iseut has succeeded in indicating her good impression of him, while at the same time making it clear that he is wrongfully persecuting her because of the evil gossip which has influenced him. Her skill with words and, no doubt, her ability as an actress to create her role as an injured innocent — she probably does not need to act her fear, although she can control and manipulate it — are used to convince Mark that he has suspected her unjustly.

This quick-wittedness, her ability to think on her feet, so to speak, and her amazing skill in manipulating words are very evident in another of the major crises of Iseut's stormy life at the court of Cornwall. Strong-minded and resourceful as she is, Beroul makes Iseut credible by showing that she can fear. Iseut has good cause to fear Mark (he was prepared to burn her at the stake and he did give her to the lepers), and when she sees his furious face after he returns from his violent quarrel with the barons, she faints (3169). It should be noted that she faints from fear for what may have happened to Tristan:

> 'Lasse', fait ele, 'mes amis
> Est trovez, mes sires l'a pris!' (3163-64)

She recovers from her faint to find that the King has been protecting her from the barons, who want her to defend herself by undergoing some form of trial by ordeal. Iseut pretends to turn to Mark for help:

> Entent a moi, si me conselle (3229)

but her own brain is already devising the answer and without waiting for Mark, she goes on:

> Se Damledeu mon cors seceure,
> Escondit mais ne lor ferai,
> Fors un que je deviserai. (3232-34)

She has already realised that she cannot take an oath, the wording of which is devised by another, whereas if she offers the oath, she is entitled to choose the formula, as is shown by Varvaro (*47*, pp.101-102). Although she has barely recovered from a shock severe enough to make her faint, she is planning swiftly and surely her escape from this next danger. As one who is offering to undergo the oath voluntarily, she is in a position to make demands and she is careful to make only reasonable ones. Arthur and his court are to be summoned (3249) to be the guarantors as they will defend her, should the verdict be challenged:

> Se devant lui sui alegie,
> Qui me voudroit aprés sordire,
> Cil me voudroient escondire,
> Qui avront veü ma deraisne,
> Vers un Cornot ou vers un Saisne. (3250-54)

Arthur appears to be an independent arbiter but as Iseut seems to know him already, he may be more committed to her than is immediately apparent:

> Son corage sai des piça. (3276)

Anyway she is quite confident that he will come to support her, and her confidence is fully borne out by subsequent events. As soon as Mark has agreed to her plan Iseut gets busy and organises Tristan. She plans his moves very fully, even reminding him to take and keep all the alms which are given to him in his disguise as a leper and bring them to her. Iseut is fond of money (see line 231 where her denial of avarice suggests that she knows that this accusation can be made against her):

> Gart moi l'argent, tant que le voie
> Priveement, en chanbre coie. (3311-12)

Her plan works brilliantly. Tristan, disguised as a leper, is waiting for her at the ford which leads to the Blanche Lande where the oath will be taken, a site chosen by Iseut, and in full view of all the onlookers she makes him carry her across the ford, riding astride him, and after dismounting she treats him with a contempt which amuses the kings and the other onlookers. It is hard to resist the conclusion that Iseut is thoroughly enjoying herself:

> Il est herlot, si que jel sai. (3976)

Her abuse makes the kings burst out laughing, but the joke is really on them and shared between Tristan and Iseut. Next day the oath is taken in public and King Arthur tells Iseut what she has to swear:

> 'Entendez moi, Yseut la bele,
> Oiez de qoi on vos apele;
> Que Tristran n'ot vers vos amor
> De puteé ne de folor
> Fors cele que devoit porter
> Envers son oncle et vers sa per.' (4191-96)

There is no way that Iseut can take that oath truthfully and the full extent of her intelligence and the skill of her planning is made clear when the audience hears her swear the oath which, as she had stipulated to Mark, she has devised:

> Or escoutez que je ci jure,
> De quoi le roi ci aseüre;
> Si m'aït Dex et saint Ylaire,
> Ces reliques, cest saintuaire,
> Totes celes qui ci ne sont
> Et tuit icil de par le mont,
> Q'entre mes cuises n'entra home,
> Fors le ladre qui fist soi some,
> Qui me porta outre les guez,
> Et li rois Marc mes esposez;
> Ces deus ost de mon soirement.
> Ge n'en ost plus de tote gent;
> De deus ne me pus escondire;
> Du ladre, du roi Marc, mon sire.
> Li ladres fu entre mes janbes
>
> . . . .
>
> Qui voudra que je plus en face,
> Tote en sui preste en ceste place. (4199-216)

She began by calling attention to the strength of her oath (4202-04), she continued with the vivid image of a man between her thighs which would capture the imagination of the audience and she then impressed them by her scrupulousness in mentioning the beggar as well as Mark, as they had all seen her astride the 'ladre'. In case anyone missed the point, she repeats that there are only these two men whom she cannot omit and then to show her confidence offers to do anything else required. The reaction is, no doubt, what she had calculated:

> Tuit cil qui l'ont oï jurer
> Ne püent pas plus endurer.
> 'Dex!' fait chascuns, 'si fiere en jure!
> Tant en a fait aprés droiture!
> Plus i a mis que ne disoient
> Ne que li fel ne requeroient (4217-22)

Iseut is vindicated on a tide of popular enthusiasm, and at last her position seems assured with Arthur and Mark satisfied. Her skill, her intelligence and her courage have carried her through this crisis to a crushing victory over her enemies.

These enemies she hates with all the strength of her passionate nature. When she has been condemned to die at the stake, her great regret is that Tristan has also been captured:

> Qui m'oceïst, si garisiez,
> Ce fust grant joie, beaus amis;
> Encor en fust vengement pris. (906-08)

When she hears that he has escaped, she is of course delighted, seeming indifferent as to whether she lives or dies:

> 'Dex,' fait elë, 'en ait bien grez!
> Or ne me chaut se il m'ocïent
> Ou il me lïent ou deslïent.' (1048-50)

It is a reasonable assumption that at least part of her delight stems from her desire for vengeance. It is not solely pleasure that Tristan has escaped. The same trait can be seen during the jousting at the ford. The forester who had betrayed the lovers falls dead from his horse, struck down by Governal:

> Yseut, qui ert et franche et sinple,
> S'en rist doucement soz sa ginple. (4055-56)

Beroul clearly approves of Iseut's attitude, as the adjective 'franche' shows, although 'sinple' is unexpected and may be used mainly for the rhyme, and there can be no arguing that she is rejoicing at the death of a dangerous enemy. At the very end of the fragment her resourcefulness and fierceness again are revealed when she carefully guides Tristan so that he can point his arrow through the hole in the curtain which Godoïne is using to spy on the lovers. She shows no squeamishness when Tristan presents her with the hair of Denoalen whom he has scalped (4390) but concentrates on the urgent business of despatching Godoïne as quickly as possible.

Iseut has a softer side to her nature although it is rarely seen. She is moved by the devotion of the dog Husdent who finds them in the forest and whom Tristan proposes to kill because his barking will betray them. It is Iseut who suggests that the dog can be trained to hunt silently and comments:

> Amis Tristran, grant joie fust,
> Por metre peine qui peüst
> Faire Hudent le cri laisier (1587-89)

The strength of her love for Tristan is also made clear more than once both before and after the potion has worn off. (The problem of the potion will be considered separately.) While the potion lasts, Beroul states categorically that the lovers can endure anything for the sake of each other:

> Aspre vie meine[n]t et dure;
> Tant s'entraiment de bone amor,
> L'un por l'autre ne sent dolor. (1364-66)

He does not minimise the hardships of life in the forest but *omnia vincit amor*. Once the potion has worn off, when one would expect the strength of their love to diminish, Beroul, less explicitly but in my opinion quite deliberately, makes it clear that although the nature of the love may have changed in that the lovers are no longer prepared to make the same sacrifices, Iseut is still very much in love. Not only does she promise to come whenever Tristan sends for her (2792-2802) whatever may be the obstacles between them, but when he finally rides away towards the sea into exile, as far as everyone knows except Iseut, she watches him until her eyes can no longer see him:

> Vers la mer vet Tristran sa voie.
> Yseut o les euz le convoie;
> Tant con de lui ot la veüe,
> De la place ne se remue. (2929-32)

For a Queen suspected of adultery who has just been received back into society by her husband, this is a bold gesture, and I would suggest that only the strength of Iseut's love could make her forget her caution.

In some ways she seems to be a selfish person. It is perhaps understandable that she shows little concern for Mark. To her he is an obstacle. Before she ever met him, she was in love with Tristan. She seems to have no qualms about living with Mark but she does not consider him at all. Nor does she always consider Tristan. When the effect of the potion wears off, it is very noticeable that Iseut's first thoughts are of herself and of her loss of status and of the responsibility of Brangien for this. It is easy to understand why Iseut should react in this way. As she points out, she is alone in the court, a foreigner and the daughter of a hated enemy, who has to think for herself as there is no-one else to do it for her. This situation must have been not uncommon as the result of diplomatic marriages. Iseut feels herself to be in danger, and as the behaviour of the barons and the dwarf proves, she is absolutely right. It is no wonder therefore that she shows herself to be hard and scheming. She feels that she is fighting for her life.

She makes use of her loneliness and position of danger to gain sympathy for herself. She is an expert at manipulating the men in her life, as both Mark and Tristan prove. Knowing that Mark loves her although she does not love him (at least we are given no reason to think that she does), she is able to exercise power over him. She takes great care to present herself as the obedient wife, well trained by her mother so that she knows how she should regard her husband's relations. As in line 21, the subjunctive in line 74 is used to create the desired effect:

> Je quidai jadis que ma mere
> Amast molt les parenz mon pere,
> Et disoit ce que la mollier
> Nen avroit ja [son] seignor chier
> Qui les parenz n'en amereit (73-77)

This is supposed to explain her apparent friendliness to Tristan. A few lines later she reminds Mark of her isolated position at his court, appealing for his sympathy:

> Tote sui sole en ceste terre. (174)

She does this again when planning her oath:

> Rois, n'ai en cest païs parent
> Qui por le mien destraignement
> En feïst gerre ne revel (3239-41)

Just as she can manipulate Mark, so she can manipulate Tristan. The most obvious example of this is at her reconciliation with Mark, where Iseut persuades Tristan to break his word, a serious matter for an honourable knight. Tristan has promised to go into exile if that should be Mark's decision:

> Ge m'en irai au roi de Frise;
> Jamais n'oras de moi parler,
> Passerai m'en outre la mer. (2610-12)

Iseut, as the time for the reconciliation approaches, is not unnaturally apprehensive. Her one sure supporter is about to go into exile while her enemies will still be at court, and she has no illusions about their probable attitude to her:

> Ges dot, quar il sont molt felon. (2827)

She uses all her art to persuade Tristan to lurk nearby at least until they see how Mark is treating her:

> Gel prié, qui sui ta chiere drue,
> Qant li rois m'avra retenue,
> Que chiés Orri le forestier
> T'alles la nuit la herbergier.
> Por moi sejorner ne t'ennuit!
> Nos i geümes mainte nuit
> En nostre lit que nos fist faire... (2815-21)

Using phrases like 'ta chiere drue', beseeching him with 'por moi', reminding him of their life together ('nos i geümes' and 'en nostre lit') she puts immense pressure on him. She continues with 'beau chiers amis' (2825), repeats twice that she is afraid (2825 and 2827), twice addresses him possessively as 'li miens amis' (2829 and 2832), and Tristan agrees at once. There can be no real struggle between his love for Iseut and his pledged word to Mark. Nor are Tristan and Mark the only men whom Iseut can influence. As already mentioned, she is confident that she can summon Arthur to her aid at the oath-taking ceremony:

> Et li mien cors est toz seürs,
> Des que verra li rois Artus
> Mon mesage, qu'il vendra ça; (3273-75)

Her confidence is fully justified. Arthur and his men will leap to the defence of such a famous beauty before they know what her request is:

> Otroi a li qant que requiers...
> Por le mesage a la plus bele
> Qui soit de ci jusq' en Tudele. (3407-10)

Beroul gives us almost no description of Iseut's beauty, which is clearly one of her weapons in controlling the men in her life. This lack of description may be because we lack the scenes in which Iseut first appears in the poem, which would be the natural place for such a description, but we are given a brief comment at the reconciliation:

> Les eulz out vers, les cheveus sors. (2888)

In all the rich robes purchased for her by the hermit she is a striking figure.

For much of the fragment Iseut must be living on her nerves and there are, of course, moments when the strain is too much for her. She faints from fear at the sight of Mark's angry face. Like Tristan she is terrified when they realise that the King had discovered them asleep in the forest:

> S'il ont poor, n'en püent mais;
> Li rois sevent fel et engrés. (2123-24)

They had such good reason to fear Mark that they quite misinterpret the signs which he had left of his visit. She weeps when she falls at the feet of the hermit on their first visit:

> Iseut au pié l'ermite plore,
> Mainte color mue en poi d'ore,
> Molt li crie merci sovent (1409-11)

Nevertheless these are only brief losses of control on her part and not to be confused with the tears of rage which she sheds when she is a prisoner, for example:

> Yseut plore, par poi n'enrage. (903)

Here the tears are only the outward sign of her fury at the

prospect of her death going unavenged, not a sign of weakness.
Iseut rarely lowers her guard and when she does, is quick to
regain control.

For all her beauty, courage and resourcefulness there are
points where Iseut does not control the action. After the lovers
have been caught by Mark and the dwarf, she remains absolutely
still and silent, while Tristan argues on her behalf and offers to
defend her. Nothing that she could say will help matters. This is
one of the moments when the affair will be settled between the
men, and she needs the strength of a man to defend her.
Similarly in the forest, Tristan, the hunter, becomes the leader.
It is Tristan who decides when they will flee to Wales (2099), and
Iseut's influence dominates only in the episode with Husdent
and when they are planning their return to court. She makes no
demur when told by Tristan that if he sends for her after their
separation:

> Dame, faites mes volentez. (2791)

Iseut knows full well that there are times and places where even a
queen as able as she is must stand back and do what she is told
by the men in her life. As a foreigner in a hostile court, as an
adulterous wife fighting to preserve her secret and her position,
Iseut is at war with the society around her. She uses her beauty,
her intelligence and her courage to survive and defeat her
enemies by controlling the men nearest to her, but she wins
through by force of character, ruthlessness and brain-power.
She is not granted any of the respect or the authority of the
courtly lady, not even by her lover.

With such a partner it would be easy for Tristan to be
overshadowed and made to look rather ridiculous, but Beroul
does not allow this to happen. Tristan is a worthy partner for
Iseut, and although she usually takes the lead, he is shown to be
intelligent and quick-thinking as well as a superb man of action.
There can be no challenging Tristan's claim to be the
outstanding knight of the Cornish court. It was he who fought
the Morholt, whom no other Cornish knight would face, as the
audience is constantly reminded (28, 136, 848, 2037-38), he it
was who defeated the dragon so that he won Iseut's hand for

Mark (2559-61), and his confidence in his own valour and prowess is shown by his demand for an 'escondit' (803) which not one of the Cornish knights is prepared to accept. Presumably they, like Tristan, believe that the Morholt's conqueror is not to be overcome by those who refused to face the Morholt, even with such a good case to fight for. Ogrin also seems sure that Tristan will win any 'escondit' and advises him to repeat his offer:

> S'il veut prendre vostre escondit,
> Si qel verront grant et petit,
> Vos li offrez a sa cort faire. (2397-99)

Further proof of Tristan's strength and physical skill can be seen in the leap from the chapel, which not even a squirrel could accomplish successfully. Even if it is accepted that Tristan had God's help in this leap, it is still an amazing feat, and the whole episode illustrates his quick-thinking opportunism, as he seizes every chance offered. Tristan is not a chivalrous knight, however. We see him joust only once, an impromptu affair at the ford, where Tristan is thought to be a fairy knight by the onlookers, and he unhorses Andret who alone takes up the challenge posed by Tristan and Governal. There is a striking contrast between the courtly appearance of the two knights, their beautiful armour, Tristan's horse with its name Bel Joeor, his 'enseigne' given by his 'bele' (as Varvaro points out (*47*, pp.182-83), the whole appearance is very reminiscent of the *Cliges* of Chrétien de Troyes 4614 ff.), and the burlesque content underlined by Iseut's private, mocking laughter (4055-56).[6] Otherwise the fighting in the book is a matter of ambushes and surprise attacks. Tristan is very skilled at this style of fighting, which probably approximates very closely to contemporary reality. It is worth noting too Tristan's skill with the bow:

> En Tristran out molt buen archier,
> Molt se sout bien de l'arc aidier. (1279-80)

By the twelfth century the bow was not regarded as a knightly weapon, although it was favoured for example in south Wales, and so this skill of Tristan's is probably a throw-back to some

[6]See also Ewert II, 247.

earlier version of the legend.

Tristan's physical qualities and courage are not in doubt, and he is not without intelligence either. He had in fact already noticed Mark in the tree before Iseut arrived at the fountain and has no trouble in following her lead to deceive Mark as to the real purpose of their meeting. His ability with words almost matches that of Iseut as he pleads with her to reconcile him with Mark, offering to prove himself by an ordeal, as no-one will accept his challenge:

> Dame, ore li dites errant
> Qu'il face faire un feu ardant,
> Et je m'en entrerai el ré;
> Se ja un poil en ai bruslé
> De la haire qu'avrai vestu,
> Si me laist tot ardoir u feu;
> Qar je sai bien n'a de sa cort
> Qui a batalle o moi s'en tort. (149-56)

His confident boasting is reminiscent of the 'gabs' of epic poetry, but his offer is not accepted. Like Iseut he plays on Mark's sympathy, recalling all that he has done for him in the past, when he alone in Cornwall was willing to stand up and fight the Morholt (135-42). By calling him 'mis oncles chiers' (143) and later in his soliloquy 'beaus oncles' (251) he is reminding Mark of their relationship and that as kindred they should stand together. His enemies he describes with the word 'losengiers' (144), with all its implications of trouble-makers. He has already suggested their aim is to isolate the King from his kindred, an apparently innocent remark which should warn the King of the threat posed to the royal family:

> Or voi je bien, si con je quit,
> Qu'il ne voudroient que o lui
> Eüst home de son linage. (123-25)

In addition to harping on his relationship to the King, Tristan paints a very pathetic picture of his own condition, apparently to move Iseut, but really for Mark's benefit. He describes himself as 'cest chaitif' (107) and later tells her:

> Engagiez est tot mon hernois (204)

After Iseut has gone, Tristan stresses his loss of status, since a knight without armour has lost the tools of his trade and is a man without worth:

> Ha! [Dex,] d'ome desatorné!
> Petit fait om de lui cherté!
> Qant je serai en autre terre,
> S'oi chevalier parler de gerre,
> Ge n'en oserai mot soner;
> Hom nu n'a nul leu de parler. (243-48)

When this is taken with his skilful denials of a guilty relationship with the Queen, it is not surprising that he succeeds in convincing Mark for the moment:

> Beaus oncles, poi me deconnut
> Qui de ta feme me mescrut;
> Onques n'oi talent de tel rage;
> Petit savroit a mon corage. (251-54)

Mark is moved to tears (262) by the pathos of the scene which he has just witnessed.

Another side of Tristan's character emerges in the scene at the ford. Iseut has told him what to do and he has carried out her instructions to the letter, but the role of the leper gives him a chance to make fun of his enemies and he takes full advantage of it. Even before the barons or the kings appear, he enjoys himself extracting alms from everyone he can:

> Tristran lor fait des borses trere,
> Que il fait tant, chascun li done (3632-33)

There is humour in the crude scuffling as Tristan drives off tormentors with his leper's crutch (3647-52). The humour is principally found, however, in his appeal to the unsuspecting Arthur, who is wheedled into giving up his gaiters (3732-34), quickly followed by his exchange with Mark, who gives him his hood and goes off laughing at the beggar's claim that his disease came from his mistress, who is almost as fair as Iseut and dresses just like her. I have already mentioned the way in which Iseut mounts the beggar and then after he has carried her safely across the ford denounces him as a sturdy rogue, refusing to give him alms as he had collected so much already. The kings are amused, but the audience can share the amusement of the lovers. Tristan's sense of mischief and malice are best shown, however, in his treatment of the barons, whom he lures into the most dangerous part of the swamp so that they are covered in mud and nearly die:

> Li felon entrent en la fange;
> La ou li ladres lor enseigne,
> Fange troverent a mervelle
> Desi q'as auves de la selle;
> Tuit troi chïent a une flote. (3797-801)

Pretending to help he offers his stick to Denoalen and then lets go so that the baron falls even further into the mud, while the leper blames his poor swollen hands (3839-52). Like Iseut, Tristan clearly enjoys playing his role, although it is a very dangerous one and his disguise is not perfect, as his friend Dinas has recognised him (3854-55). Nevertheless Tristan plays his part with such panache that no-one else suspects a thing, and it is evident that he enjoys the danger as a challenge.

He has a nicer side to his nature too. When the effect of the potion wears off, Tristan does think of both the Queen and his uncle. He is sorry for the suffering which has been caused. To be sure he starts off by regretting the three years lost in the forest and thinking of his own lost position:

> Oublié ai chevalerie
> A seure cort et baronie (2165-66)

He soon does think of his uncle:

> Dex! tant m'amast mes oncle(r)s chiers,
> Se tant ne fuse a lui mesfez! (2170-71)

He also thinks of Iseut, whom he refers to formally as 'la roïne':

> Et poise moi de la roïne. (2179)

His aim now is to seek a reconciliation between husband and wife:

> A Deu vo je que jel feroie
> Molt volentiers, se je pooie,
> Si que Yseut fust acordee
> O le roi Marc, qui'st esposee (2189-92)

It is not surprising that Tristan should be more concerned with

Mark than Iseut ever is, because as he himself remembers, they are uncle and nephew. There are, presumably, old bonds of affection between them which the disappearance of the potion allows to reappear. Tristan is also always willing to sacrifice himself for Iseut, as can be seen when he breaks his word to go into exile and instead goes and stays at Orri's house, while the lovers wait to see how Mark will behave to Iseut. Similarly, once he has escaped by jumping from the chapel, Tristan is concerned with nothing but the rescue of Iseut and indeed has to be restrained by Governal from rushing uselessly back into the town in search of her, where he would be overwhelmed by the numbers of his enemies. He is also conscious of his rank, for all that during their exile in the forest he, like Iseut, is ready to lead a life of unparalleled harshness. Not only does he immediately think of his lost rank and status when the potion wears off, but Beroul makes a point of telling us that Tristan was too noble to soil himself by killing the lepers:

> Trop ert Tristran preuz et cortois
> A ocirre gent de tes lois. (1269-70)

He shows considerable pride and independence in refusing to accept any money from Mark for his exile:

> Tristran dist; 'Rois de Cornoualle,
> Ja n'en prendrai mie maalle' (2923-24)

He might also feel some reluctance to accept money from a man to whom he is just about to break a promise.

Quick-witted and opportunistic like Iseut, Tristan has no great difficulty in holding his own in a very dangerous society. The reckless streak in his character which can be seen in the scene at the ford, where he enjoys himself by teasing Mark with his reference to his mistress, almost as beautiful as Iseut, is also seen much earlier in the poem, when he leaps to Iseut's bed to take his pleasure although he knows that the dwarf is setting a trap for them, because he has seen him scattering flour on the floor. His passion is so great that he thinks that he can outwit the dwarf by leaping from bed to bed, another example of his tremendous physical skill and strength. This reckless streak shows itself only rarely, but it is certainly there and helps perhaps to explain both why Tristan is such a hero and why he seems to enjoy danger. His scorn for the Cornish who were afraid of the Morholt is very telling:

> Molt les vi ja taisant et muz,
> Qant li Morhot fu ça venuz,
> Ou nen i out uns d'eus tot sous
> Qui osast prendre ses adous. (135-38)

He is a very attractive character, more attractive perhaps than Iseut, although her impact on the reader is probably the greater.

3. *King Mark and the minor characters*

The most important of the other characters is King Mark, who is a very complex personality in Beroul. His problem is that he is deeply in love with Iseut:

> Qar sa feme forment amot. (2520)

He is also very fond of Tristan, as his plea when Tristan vanishes after delivering the letter suggests:

> Por Deu, beaus niés, ton oncle atent! (2473)

As Varvaro shows (*47*, pp.167-68), it is this love, often resulting in compassion, which saves him from the ungrateful rule of the comic, cuckolded husband of the *fabliaux*. He is, however, haunted by the fear, at times the certainty, that his nephew and his wife are lovers, and his character is crisply summed up by Perinis:

> Li rois n'a pas coraige entier,
>
> Senpres est ci et senpres la. (3432-33)

Mark is not a very strong character, and he is caught between two strong opposing forces, the lovers on the one hand and the barons on the other. He desperately wants to believe the best of his wife and his nephew for the reasons already mentioned, but because of the lovers' reckless behaviour the barons succeed in convincing him that Tristan really is Iseut's lover. The skilful acting of the lovers in the opening scene of the fragment, where Tristan apparently begs Iseut to act as an intermediary for him with Mark, while she plays the role of the frightened, innocent wife, coupled with his desire to believe the best, makes him change his mind completely. He is convinced by the clever double-talk of the lovers to the extent that he is in tears at the end of the scene and ready to turn on those who persuaded him into the tree:

> Molt het le nain de Tintaguel. (264)

He decides that Tristan will no longer be banned from the royal bed-chamber and with deep, unconscious irony says:

> Molt est fous qui croit tote gent. (308)

It is impossible not to feel some flicker of sympathy for this desperately worried man who at this point in the poem wants to do the right thing and has been deceived by the brilliant acting of two people whom he wants to believe innocent, acting which they are able to sustain throughout the subsequent interview when he confronts Iseut with the query:

> Dame, veïs puis mon nevo? (399)

She tells him the truth which he had seen and heard for himself and so he is completely reassured and ready to welcome back Tristan, all the more so as Brangien is able to give him an opportunity to appear magnanimous by inventing a quarrel between herself and Tristan which Mark is able to resolve by offering to forgive Tristan if Tristan will forgive Brangien. He does not notice the lack of interest in the quarrel on the part of Tristan, as he is only too happy to accede to Tristan's request that there should be a general reconciliation between husband, wife and nephew.

His weakness and his readiness to believe the last speaker are obvious shortly afterwards when, in spite of his declared belief in the innocence of Tristan and Iseut (287) and his lack of belief in the barons (288), he listens all too readily to their new accusations:

> Li rois l'entent, fist un sospir,
> Son chief abesse vers la terre,
> Ne set qu'il die, sovent erre. (610-12)

Seeing his irresolution they threaten to leave the court and make war on him (621-22), and Mark, as his feudal role requires, seeks their advice, but his words sound weak and uncertain, revealing the pathetic side of his character as he is torn between his duty as a king and his feelings for his family:

> Conseliez m'en, gel vos requier;
> Vos me devez bien consellier,
> Que servise perdre ne vuel. (631-33)

As a result of the barons' advice to recall the dwarf, the lovers are caught almost *in flagrante delicto*, and Mark reacts with all the violence of a weak man who has found his trust betrayed.

Certain of the lovers' guilt he will hear no plea in their defence:

> 'Trop par a ci veraie enseigne;
> Provez estes,' ce dist li rois,
> 'Vostre escondit n'i vaut un pois.
> Certes, Tristran, demain ce quit,
> Soiez certains d'estre destruit.' (778-82)

He ignores the pleas of the common people, who look on Tristan with gratitude and Iseut with love and admiration. His fury at the escape of Tristan is great:

> De mautalent en devint noir,
> De duel ne set con se contienge (1068-69)

The intervention of Dinas the seneschal, who was in charge of justice, arguing that the summary execution of the Queen would be neither just nor politically wise serves only to increase his fury:

> Li rois prist par la main Dinas,
> Par ire a juré saint Thomas
> Ne laira n'en face justise
> Et qu'en ce fu ne soit la mise. (1125-28)

The climax comes when Mark hands Iseut over to the lepers, accepting their argument that with them her life and death will be more horrible than anything that he could devise. Iseut's claim that she would sooner be burned seals her fate. Mark will have his revenge.

Although he may be a weak character, he is not a physical coward. When the forester announces that he has discovered the lovers asleep in the forest, Mark takes his sword and goes alone, prepared to fight Tristan, a younger and presumably a stronger man. Decisive for once, he brushes aside the protests of his men with a story about going to meet a girl. He goes expecting trouble:

> Quar, se Tristran fust esvelliez,
> Li niés o l'oncle se meslast,
> Li uns morust, ainz ne finast. (1966-68)

Although distressed originally by the forester's revelation (1895-96), Mark is thoroughly roused by the time he reaches the 'loge' and having shed his cloak, cuts a fine figure of a man as he enters with drawn sword vowing vengeance:

> Li rois deslace son mantel,
>
> Dont a fin or sont li tasel;
>
> Desfublez fu, molt out gent cors.
>
> Du fuerre trait l'espee fors,
>
> Iriez s'en torne, sovent dit
>
> Q'or veut morir s'il nes ocit.
>
> L'espee nue, an la loge entre. (1981-87)

Poised to strike (1991) he suddenly sees the naked sword between the lovers, and instantly recognising this symbol of chastity (although the sword had been put there by Tristan for quite other reasons) is struck with doubt:

> Dex! je ne sai que doie faire,
>
> Ou de l'ocire ou du retraire. (2003-04)

His inner debate is brief, as once again he wants to believe them innocent, and he quickly decides to withdraw leaving them asleep to avoid the combat which he had previously been seeking:

> Se par moi eirent atouchié,
>
> Trop par feroie grant pechié;
>
> Et se g'esvel cest endormi
>
> Et il m'ocit ou j'oci lui,
>
> Ce sera laide reparlance. (2015-19)

His affection for the lovers (already shown for Tristan at line 1472 when the distress of Husdent makes him think of Tristan and his worth as a knight) resurfaces and with the best of intentions he decides to leave tokens of his visit which he hopes will make his intentions clear:

> Je lor ferai tel demostrance
>
> Ançois que il s'esvelleront,
>
> Certainement savoir porront
>
> Qu'il furent endormi trové
>
> Et q'en a eü d'eus pité,
>
> Que je nes vuel noient ocire,
>
> Ne moi ne gent de mon enpire. (2020-26)

It is not his fault that the lovers completely misinterpret his gesture, Iseut waking in terror from her nightmare when the gloves, so thoughtfully left to shield her face, fall on her breast.

Her fear communicates itself to Tristan and remembering their previous experience of Mark, they conclude that he has gone for help (2096-98).

As Mark again believes the evidence of his own eyes and is therefore convinced of the innocence of the lovers, he is well-disposed to the suggestion of a reconciliation. Indeed it looks as if he will welcome both lovers back to court, but as ever he listens to the barons and in the end after some hesitation, despite the advice of Andret, he sends Tristan into exile. The barons succeeded in changing his mind by their references to Iseut:

> La roïne a esté blasmee
> Et foï hors de ta contree.
> Se a ta cort resont ensenble,
> Ja dira l'en, si con nos senble,
> Que en consent lor felonie. (2895-99)

Mark escorts Tristan on his way, and it is noticeable that with Tristan exiled Mark seems to become more confident. Mark believes that Tristan has gone and so he is sure that there can be no affair, whatever there may have been in the past. As a result, when the barons resume their campaign against Iseut, Mark turns on them with the ferocity which he had shown to Tristan and Iseut after the dwarf had trapped them:

> Li rois les a si esfreez
> Qu'il n'i a el fors prengent fuie. (3080-81)

In a speech of great violence, in the course of which he calls on God, 'saint Estiene le martir' and 'seint Tresmor de Caharés' as well as cursing the jaw of those who 'me rova de lui partir' (3069), he bitterly reminds the barons of their failure to accept Tristan's challenge in the past, their part in deciding Tristan's exile, and their hostility to Mark's interests. His rage is conveyed by the breathless syntax:

> Lui ai chacie; or chaz ma feme? (3067)

and by the incoherence observable in the climax where he threatens to recall Tristan:

> '[...]
> Ge vos ferai un geu parti;
> Ainz ne verroiz passé marsdi —

Hui est lundi — si le verrez.' (3077-79)

In spite of their efforts to appease him he orders them away:

Or gerpisiez tote ma terre. (3131)

His fury is misinterpreted by Iseut who faints with fear that he has caught Tristan. She does after all have a guilty conscience and so misinterprets his behaviour just as she did when she awoke in the 'loge' to find his gloves. Despite his fury Mark could not be kinder as she, after all, is not the target of his wrath:

Q'entre ses braz l'en a levee,

Besie l'a et acolee (3171-72)

When she agrees to take the oath, he is willing, but there is no sign of any pressure on his part to make her take one, whatever the barons may say. He behaves with great kindness to the beggar at the ford, giving him his hood (3749-52) and laughing at his joke, not realising the cruel irony which is aimed at him (3769-77). His confidence can also be seen in the way in which he accepts Arthur's criticisms of his conduct:

Tu me blasmes, et si as droit,

Quar fous est qui envieus croit;

Ges ai creüz outre mon gré. (4171-73)

He admits frankly that he was in the wrong and so avoids the appearance of weakness. His role at the oath-taking ceremony is small, as Arthur presides, but when it is over Beroul makes clear that Mark has established his authority:

Li rois a Cornoualle en pes,

Tuit le criement et luin et pres;

En ses deduiz Yseut en meine,

De lié amer forment se paine. (4267-70)

Both as a King and a husband Mark's position seems secure. The audience, of course, shares the author's knowledge that Mark's confidence and happiness are illusory.

Beroul's picture of Mark is not unsympathetic, but to a medieval audience any cuckold was a figure of fun and, although Mark is too dangerous to be regarded with amusement by either the lovers or the barons, there are two scenes in which a trace of this attitude can be seen. In the opening scene of the fragment when Mark is up in the tree, he has little of the dignity of a king, and his readiness to be convinced is both comic and pathetic. The audience are involved with the lovers and sympathise with their successful outwitting of the injured husband. Any feeling of amusement disappears of course in subsequent scenes where Mark shows how dangerous and vindictive he can be. The episode of the horse's ears reduces the tension. That is presumably one of the reasons for its presence. Beroul's audience would enjoy the change of tone, and the slackening of the tension is necessary after the drama of the arrest and escape of the lovers. The story itself reflects the influences of folktale, Celtic literature and classical literature. The parallel with King Midas is obvious, and in Welsh *march* meant a horse. The audience would be familiar with the idea that someone who bore the name of an animal had a special relationship with it, and given that the dwarf seems to have special knowledge of Mark's problem (1307-08), it would be quite easy for them to accept that with a necromancer like the dwarf to help him, Mark had been a shape-shifter, able to adopt the shape of the animal whose name he shared. He had taken on the shape of his beast but had not been completely successful in retransforming himself. Beroul does not spell this out, but in an age where belief in the occult was more widespread than our own, he did not need to. His audience would understand and would accept that the dwarf deserved his fate for being both indiscreet and inefficient. Mark is clearly an object of some ridicule but the ruthless way in which he disposes of the dwarf soon checks any smiles.

Mark emerges as a not unlikeable character, for all that he has such an ungrateful role. His love for Iseut and his affection for Tristan are clear and do much to explain the violence of his reaction, as nothing is worse than to find trust and affection betrayed. Beroul's Mark cares deeply for his wife and his nephew. The hurt caused to him is correspondingly great, and Beroul takes care to make this clear to the audience. Mark is too fierce and dangerous to be a figure of fun, but is generally recognised to be weak and unpredictable. Nevertheless once

Tristan is away from court, Mark seems more assured and relaxed, as at last his mind is at rest. Although he accepts Arthur's rebuke, he is not in awe of him and is not his vassal. Beroul is probably fairer and kinder to Mark than are the other authors of the Tristan legend.

None of the minor characters rivals Mark in importance. Arthur appears in the second part of the poem as the guarantor of Iseut at the oath-taking ceremony. He had already been mentioned early in the fragment, as Mark had used the pretext of an urgent message to Arthur at Carduel (Carlisle) to set the trap for the lovers (684-85). Mark seems to regard Arthur as an equal, and later Perinis is sent to find him on behalf of Iseut at Isneldone (3373), which is almost certainly not Stirling as is frequently claimed but more likely to be in North Wales.[7] Perinis goes by Cuerlion (Caerleon on Usk) (3368) and then is guided by a shepherd, typical of the pastoral society of twelfth century Wales, to the Round Table:

> Ja verroiz la Table Reonde,
> Qui tornoie conme le monde (3379-80)

Beroul has clearly heard of this marvellous object linked with Arthur, and as far as we know first associated with Arthur by Wace in c.1155, but equally clearly he does not seem very sure of its nature. Nor does he give any description of the buildings where Arthur has his court. The suggestion that in fact the description of Arthur in Beroul is based on one of the near-nomadic Welsh chieftains of the period is convincing.[8] Placing Arthur in Wales would also explain how Perinis was able to find him and how Arthur was able to come within the fourteen days stipulated by Mark (3279) as a reasonable period for arranging the oath. If Isneldone is Stirling, such a journey would be quite impossible, and some at least of Beroul's audience would know this.

Arthur himself is a lively, tough-minded character, clearly in control of his court, who reacts immediately and generously to

[7] Miss E.M.R. Ditmas, 'King Arthur in Beroul's *Tristan*', unpublished paper delivered at the Cardiff meeting of the International Arthurian Society in 1969.
[8] Ibid.

Iseut's call for help:

> Vaslet, voiant cest mien barnage,
> Otroi a li qant que requiers. (3406-07)

He offers to knight Perinis on the spot, and after Perinis has delivered his message, his knights follow the example of their leader and vie with one another in the fierceness of their threats against the three barons, a feature which links Beroul to the epic tradition where such *gabs* are usual. Arthur makes no enquiry as to the nature of the affair. For him it is enough that the beautiful Iseut, whom he seems to know already (through Perinis she calls herself his 'chiere amie' (3438)) has called for help. For all that his style of life shows little sign of sophisticated courtly influence (there is no mention of the presence of ladies, and his court seems to be simple), he behaves towards Iseut as if he knew something of the conventions of courtly society. He is moved by her beauty, he assumes that she is in the right and he promises to be at her disposal:

> Totes ferai ses volentez (3543)

When he arrives at the ford with his suite, he shows pity to the leper begging there and gives his gaiters as requested, finding considerable amusement in the exchanges between first Mark and the leper and then Iseut and the leper. He enjoys the company of Iseut:

> Artus la roïne destroie,
> Molt li senbla brive la voie... (4075-76)

His strong personality means that he takes charge of the ceremony, and Beroul does suggest that it is by force of character that he takes control. There is no hint that Mark is his vassal but he seems to be the more important king:

> Li rois Artus parla premier,
> Qui de parler fu prinsautier (4139-40)

He firmly rebukes Mark for his failure to control the barons, and Mark accepts his right to do so. Arthur and his household clearly dominate the ceremony with Gauvain next to the relics, and it is Arthur who tells Iseut the oath which she is to take (see p.22). Like everyone else he is the dupe of her apparently excessive honesty, and at the end of the scene he threatens the barons with all his power if they dare to trouble her again. The situation settled to his satisfaction, Arthur departs to Durham (4264).

There seems to be no bond between Mark and Arthur except that of the friendship of two neighbouring kings. Mark accepts that Arthur is the stronger character, who perhaps sees more clearly than he does, so that he is prepared to follow Arthur's advice, but there is no suggestion in the fragment that Mark is Arthur's vassal. Arthur behaves differently from the Cornish, treating the lady with respect, but then he is an outsider not involved in the feuds of the Cornish court. His court seems to be just as masculine a stronghold as the Cornish court, and it is hard to see more than a superficial veneer of courtly behaviour there in the unquestioning assumption that the beautiful Iseut must be in the right. He is a contrast to Mark, providing an example of a strong, forceful ruler and, because he is on the side of the lovers, Beroul presents him sympathetically, but he remains a minor character passing quickly through the poem when the lovers need him.

The other characters whom Beroul chooses to individualise divide into the supporters and the enemies of the lovers. Governal and Perinis, who are the squires of Tristan and Iseut respectively, are whole-hearted supporters of their master and mistress. Perinis is the messenger between the lovers, he is present in the room, asleep at the foot of the bed when Tristan and Iseut are caught. Very sensibly, he remains still and does not get involved (764). Beroul approves of him, as his description shows when forecasting the death of the forester:

> Quar Perinis, li franc, li blois,
> L'ocist puis d'un gibet el bois. (2761-62)

He behaves well on his visit to Arthur, who offers to knight him, but the offer is gracefully declined. As already mentioned, he is shrewd enough to be able to sum up Mark's character and explain the reason for the present troubles at the court. At the end of the fragment he is again present in the Queen's bedroom when she directs Tristan to kill Godoïne. A shrewd, pleasant young man, well able to hold his own in the rough world of the

Cornish court, Perinis never wavers in his devotion to Iseut.

Governal's first loyalty is to Tristan. He is an older man for whom Tristan has considerable respect:

> Qant il [Tristan] le vit, grant joie en fait.
> 'Maistre, ja m'a Dex fait merci (978-79)

This title of 'maistre' indicates the relationship between them. Governal seems to be the tutor and advisor of Tristan. He is certainly completely committed to Tristan. He knows that he can expect no mercy from Mark:

> Bien set, se il fust conseüz,
> Li rois l'arsist por son seignor (968-69)

He is shrewd, capable and cool. He has the foresight to take Tristan's sword with him to help Tristan should he escape (972-73). He is the one who restrains Tristan from rushing uselessly into the town in a forlorn attempt to rescue Iseut. He disposes of the leper Ivain, when Tristan cannot bring himself to soil his hands with such filth:

> Governal est venuz au cri,
> En sa main tint un vert jarri
> Et fiert Yvain, qui Yseut tient;
> Li sans li chiet, au pié li vie[n]t.
> Bien aïde a Tristran son mestre,
> Yseut saisist par la main destre. (1259-64)

He accompanies the lovers into the forest of Morrois, where he is responsible for the cooking:

> Governal sot de la cuisine. (1294)

Governal lies in wait for one of the barons and decapitates him in the forest when he has been separated from the rest of his hunting party. In the scene at the ford Governal is lying in hiding with arms and horses for Tristan when he decides to abandon his disguise, and they ride down together spreading consternation among the knights, who see them as other-wordly beings (4019). While Tristan jousts with Andret and breaks his arm, Governal kills the forester, who falls dead before Iseut to her great delight. He is constantly with Tristan, as the spy who warns the barons of Tristan's continued presence in Cornwall has seen them together (4299). His loyalty and devotion to Tristan are his outstanding features but he too is a tough, competent follower, whose presence of mind and physical prowess undoubtedly help the lovers when they need him.

Dinas is a slightly different case. He is Mark's seneschal and as such responsible for the administration of justice, and presumably his first loyalty ought to be to Mark. From his very first appearance, however, it is made clear that he is a supporter of Tristan:

> Dinas, li sire de Dinan,
>
> Qui a mervelle amoit Tristran (1085-86)

He resists the execution of the Queen on legal grounds:

> Vos la volez sanz jugement
>
> Ardoir en feu; ce n'est pas gent,
>
> Qar cest mesfait ne connoist pas (1097-99)

He is also aware of good practical reasons for caution. Tristan is free and dangerous. He will certainly seek vengeance for the death of a woman who means so much to him:

> Mais vos barons, en sa ballie
>
> S'il les trovout, nes vilonast,
>
> Encor en ert ta terre en gast. (1106-08)

Pleading his loyalty, he begs the King to entrust Iseut to him:

> Rois, rent la moi, par la merite
>
> Que servi t'ai tote ma vite. (1119-20)

He has already reminded the King of his incorruptibility, of which he is justifiably proud:

> Ja n'avras home en tot cest reigne,
>
> Povre orfelin ne vielle feme,
>
> Qui por vostre seneschaucie,
>
> Que j'ai eü tote ma vie,
>
> Me donast une beauveisine. (1091-95)

Despite the demands of justice and expediency the King in his fury swears to carry out the penalty, and Dinas withdraws from court with dignity, refusing at any price to see Iseut burnt (1133-39). During the exile of the lovers he must be reconciled with Mark, as he reappears at court to urge that the letter from Tristan be heard (2539), and subsequently he accompanies Mark at the reconciliation, riding with him in front of the rest of the Cornish (2845-47). It is his task to escort the Queen and entertain her while the decision is taken about exiling Tristan:

> La roïne ovoc Dinas let,
> Qui molt par ert voirs et loiaus
> Et d'anor faire conmunax.
> O la roïne geue et gabe (2876-79)

Once the decision has been taken, Dinas escorts Tristan as he rides away and at Tristan's urgent request promises to do whatever Tristan requires:

> Dinas li prie ja nel dot,
> Die son buen; il fera tot. (2945-46)

He it is who hands Iseut the gift which she dedicates in the church of St Samson. Beroul's approval is clear from the description of him:

> Dinas li preuz, qui molt fu ber (2984)

This is another of the lines which show Beroul's familiarity with epic, as the terms used could come straight from the description of an epic hero. He reappears as the Queen's escort at the ford, where he alone recognises Tristan (3855), and warns the Queen of the danger to her clothes when crossing the ford. After the oath-taking ceremony it is with Dinas that Tristan and Governal find shelter and safety until they are discovered by the spy.

As Ewert says, 'Dinas, seneschal of King Mark, is the most consistently attractive figure in Beroul's romance' (*1*, II, 145). He is upright and tries to combine loyalty to Mark with friendship for Tristan, since he realises that the King's best interests are not served by quarrelling with his nephew. For Tristan's sake he is fond of Iseut and sees to it that she is treated with dignity at the reconciliation. He must know that he is supporting an adulterous love affair, but he is prepared to do so in what he sees as a higher cause, the need for Cornwall to be well governed by Mark, which can best be achieved by the combination of Mark and Tristan, for Mark needs Tristan to support him against his rebellious and difficult barons. In the swirling passions and enmities of the Cornish court Dinas is perhaps the only character to try to take a long-term view.

The only female character of any importance apart from Iseut is Brangien. She is whole-hearted in her support of the lovers, no doubt because she was genuinely devoted to them, but also perhaps because she had a guilty conscience, as it was through her folly that the mistake happened and they drank the potion:

> Ce fist Brengain, qu'i dut garder. (2208)

Iseut has no doubt where the blame lies. Brangien's role is small, however, compared with her importance in some of the other versions. She has one big scene near the beginning of the fragment and thereafter is seen only with Iseut watching the jousting and carrying Iseut's comb as she and Perinis attend the Queen in her room. Iseut treats her with some respect, calling her 'magistre' (345), an indication that she has the status of a confidante as well as that of lady-in-waiting. Brangien knows at once from Iseut's face that things have gone wrong but she rejoices whole-heartedly in Iseut's quickness; she too sees God's hand at work:

> Quant l'ot Brengain, molt s'en esjot;
>   'Iseut, ma dame, grant merci
> Nos a Dex fait, qui ne menti
> [...]' (370-72)

She is quick-witted and cunning too. To help Mark achieve a reconciliation with Tristan, she pretends that she is afraid to go to Tristan as they have quarrelled. Beroul is full of admiration for her skill:

> Oiez que dit la tricherresse!
> Molt fist que bone lecherresse (519-20)

Mark agrees to reconcile them, thus appearing magnanimous, and Brangien goes to fetch Tristan. She too has duped Mark, but the whole excuse is quickly forgotten as Tristan concentrates on his own grievances. Subtle and lively Brangien is a fit companion to Iseut and ably seconds her when she has the opportunity.

The last and least important character in this group is Andret, who also poses the biggest problem. He appears first of all at the reconciliation scene, where he is presented as the King's nephew from Lincoln. He seems therefore to be Tristan's cousin (although 'neveu' and 'cousin' are not always used with strict accuracy in Old French):

> Li rois a son nevo parole.
> Andrez, qui fu nez de Nicole,
> Li a dit; 'Rois, quar le retiens,
> Plus en seras doutez et criens.' (2869-72)

As might be expected, Andret is supporting his cousin and urging Mark to keep him at court. The implication is that the family will be strengthened. His advice almost prevails:

> Molt en faut poi que ne l'otroie,
> Le cuer forment l'en asouploie. (2873-74)

The three barons intervene (2893-906), however, and the King accepts their advice. There is no reason to see Andret as anything other than an ally of the lovers. He next appears crossing the ford with Dinas (3877), leaving Iseut on the same side as the beggar. Again there is nothing to suggest that the lovers find him a nuisance. His final brief appearance is when he alone of all the knights takes up the challenge posed by Tristan, whom he has not recognised, and rides out to joust with this seemingly fairy opponent. (Although 'faé' (4019) need not mean supernatural, there is no reason to reject Ewert's translation of 'enchanted' here. Tristan and Governal are thought to be otherworldly beings.)

> [...] Et Andrez vint
> Sor son destrier, ses armes tint;
> Lance levee, l'escu pris,
> A Tristran saut en mié le vis.
> Nu connoisoit de nule rien,
> Et Tristran le connoisoit bien;
> Fiert l'en l'escu, en mié la voie
> L'abat et le braz li peçoie.
> Devant les piez a la roïne
> Cil jut sanz lever sus l'eschine (4035-44)

Beroul does not say that Andret is dead. He is wounded in the arm and perhaps unconscious after the fall from his horse; if his state is compared with that of the forester which follows immediately afterwards, it is easy to see the difference. There

can be no arguing that the forester is dead and that Iseut is
delighted about it:

> Le fer trenchant li mist el cors,
> O l'acier bote le cuir fors.
> Cil chaï mort, si c'onques prestre
> N'i vint a tens ne n'i pot estre.
> Yseut, qui ert et franche et sinple,
> S'en rist doucement soz sa ginple. (4051-56)

If the argument is accepted that Andret is not dead and that
Tristan probably took care not to kill him (a knight of Tristan's
standing would surely have been able to kill his opponent if he
had really wanted to), the problem disappears. It had always
been puzzling that Andret of Lincoln, who seems to be so well
disposed towards the lovers, should be treated by Tristan like an
enemy. It was suggested that there were two Andrets, the one of
Lincoln who was well disposed and another one who was not. It
was also seen as evidence for the two Berouls, as the second
Beroul could have forgotten how the first one treated Andret. In
fact it seems more likely that it is the same person throughout.
As the King's nephew he would be the obvious person to take up
the challenge of a stranger. Tristan has recognised him and
inflicts a wound on him which is not particularly serious. Iseut
shows no emotion either way at his defeat. The character is
consistent; a supporter of the lovers and a brave and honourable
knight.

The enemies of the lovers consist of the dwarf Frocin and the
barons. Of these the dwarf is by far the most dangerous
(medieval dwarves are often evil, as can be seen in the romances
of Chrétien de Troyes), and it is noticeable that the lovers gain
the upper hand completely only after the death of the dwarf. He
is described as 'le nain de Tintaguel' (264), and it was he who
persuaded Mark up into the tree to spy on the lovers. He is a
skilled astrologer (321-330) and is able to read in the stars that
his plans have failed and that the King has changed sides. Like
the lovers later in the poem he flees 'vers Gales' (336), meaning
presumably to the north coast of Cornwall to take ship across
the Bristol Channel to Wales. He is filled with anger and spite

(*mautalent*, 332) at this. Beroul is bitterly opposed to this character and makes sure that the audience is left in no doubt about the proper attitude to him:

> Dehez ait il conme boçuz! (640)

and

> Con fist cist nain, qui Dex maudie (648)

His communications with the barons are good, for as soon as Mark wavers at all, the barons persuade him to recall Frocin, who returns with a very dangerous plan all worked out. He is sure that Tristan's lust and overconfidence will lead to his downfall and he is proved correct. The author can scarcely restrain his indignation:

> Molt fu li nain de grant voidie,
> Molt par fist rede felonie [...]
> Qui pensast mais tel traïson? (673-78)

The trap works. The lovers are in bed together, and the dwarf is on the watch outside:

> Li nains defors est; a la lune
> Bien vit josté erent ensenble
> Li dui amant; de joie en trenble (736-38)

His delight in his success makes him seem more odious than ever. He runs in with the barons, holding the candle for them, and is execrated by the people for his part in the downfall of the lovers (842-43). He alone amongst the Cornish rejoices (879-80). He then disappears from the poem until the episode of the horse's ears. The dwarf is the only one to know this secret of the King, and one day when he is drunk (1311) the barons want to know why he and the King confer so much together. He will not tell them and break his word, but instead he whispers the secret into a hole in the ground, having arranged with the barons for them to overhear. The secret is out, but Mark reacts with considerable sang-froid:

> Li rois s'en rist et dist: 'Ce mal,
> Que j'ai orelles de cheval,
> M'est avenu par cest devin;
> Certes ja ert de lui fin.'
> Traist l'espee, le chief en prent. (1343-47)

The dwarf has got his just reward as Mark blames him for the disfigurement and also for his treachery. Everyone is delighted that the enemy of Tristan and Iseut is dead:

> Molt en fu bel a mainte gent,
> Que haoient le nain Frocine
> Por Tristran et por la roïne. (1348-50)

The role of Frocin would be no surprise to the medieval audience. Beroul takes care to make him the personification of malice, with a mind as deformed as his body (a common medieval belief). Clever and ruthless, the dwarf is by far the greatest threat to the lovers, but his own folly and pride bring about his downfall, just as he had used Tristan's folly and overconfidence to trap him. With his death the barons have lost their ablest agent.

The number of the barons is one of the great problems in Beroul. He mentions them for the first time in the fragment as three (we have no way of knowing whether or not this is their first appearance in the poem, but they are referred to by Iseut in line 26 without individualising them):

> A la cort avoit trois barons,
> Ainz ne veïstes plus felons (581-82)

From the first mention it is clear how the audience is meant to see them. There are three evil men at the court who are the declared enemies of Tristan and Iseut. One of them is subsequently ambushed and decapitated by Governal in the forest (1711), but when Beroul 'prophesies' the deaths of the enemies of the lovers (2755-64), there are still three barons as well as the forester, two to be killed by swords, one by an arrow, and the forester by Perinis. The problem of the forester will be looked at separately, but, as regards the barons, it seems possible that Beroul regarded the number three as important and so, although one baron had been killed already, another had been recruited in his place (see *30*, pp.149-50). After all, Tristan was not short of enemies. The other explanations are that Beroul forgot that he had already killed one of the barons or that the second Beroul had taken over by this point, hence the confusion.

Even without the dwarf the barons are dangerous enemies.

Despite Andret's advice they manage to persuade the King to send Tristan into exile for a year. They had been poised ready to intervene should Mark weaken (2892). They miscalculate, however, when they try again to persuade Mark that Iseut should take an 'escondit' (3043). Mark's mind is now at peace as Tristan is not at court, and his quick temper reacts violently to their intervention. The text suggests that Mark is feeling guilty about his treatment of Tristan. He abuses the barons roundly, reminding them of all that Tristan did which they had not dared to do, saying that they are responsible for his exile and threatening to recall him immediately. His scorn is clear:

> N'offri Tristran li a defendre?
>
> Ainz n'en osastes armes prendre. (3063-64)

The barons are frightened by his fury, betraying their cowardice, as Mark curses them.

> [...] Dex vos destruie,
>
> Qui si alez querant ma honte! (3082-83)

They make an attempt to pacify him, claiming to be counselling (3112-13), but Mark will have none of them and rides away. They withdraw to their castles and their real feelings emerge:

> A lor seignor feront ennui,
>
> Se la chose n'est amendee. (3146-47)

It was, of course, a most grave offence to make war on one's feudal overlord. They are, however, too powerful to be ignored. Mark refers to them as 'Trois de mes plus proisiez barons' (3219). Iseut sees her chance here to be freed from their mischief-making for ever, by summoning Arthur and his men to witness her oath. At Arthur's court they are at last identified as Godoïne, Guenelon and Denoalen, all traitors well known at that court whom Arthur's men would love to destroy. They are mocked and made to look ridiculous by Tristan at the ford, and after the oath has been sworn successfully by Iseut Arthur is unsparing in his threats and condemnation:

> Or esgardent li troi felon,
>
> Donoalent et Guenelon,
>
> Et Goudoïne li mauvés,
>
> Qu(e) il ne parolent sol jamés. (4237-40)

The three, however, have no intention of living in peace. Their
spies are still at work:

> Mais, qui q'ait pais, li troi felon
> Sont en esgart de traïson.
> A eus fu venue une espie (4271-73)

Thanks to him they know that it is possible to spy on the lovers
in the Queen's bedroom and it is decided that Godoïne should go
first. In fact Tristan sees him en route and sets an ambush which
Godoïne by chance avoids, but instead Denoalen is caught and
scalped by Tristan, who is then guided by Iseut to shoot Godoïne
through the curtain in her room. Only Guenelon is left and his
death has been foretold.

Beroul makes little attempt to differentiate between the
barons, who are usually shown as a unit. Arthur's knights
distinguish slightly between them. According to Gauvain:

> Li plus coverz est Guenelons. (3462)

The clear onomastic allusion to the traitor of the *Chanson de
Roland* is certainly in line with this remark. Yvain picks out
Denoalen and describes him as a skilled intriguer:

> Asez connois Dinoalen;
> Tot son sens met en acuser,
> Bien set faire le roi muser (3484-86)

Girflet adds little to the description of Godoïne.

No effort is spared by Beroul to blacken the barons. As they
themselves point out, they are carrying out their feudal duty of
counselling their lord. Since the Queen is betraying her husband,
his honour is at stake and anyone guilty of adultery with the
Queen is committing treason. Beroul allows none of this to
count. The barons may be carrying out their feudal duty but
their motives are bad. Jealousy, envy, fear and hatred drive
them on against the lovers. They see the presence of the lovers at
court as a threat to their position, as Tristan and Iseut are their
rivals for Mark's ear. When Tristan is not there, Mark listens to
them, but when he and Iseut are at court, the influence of the
barons is challenged. They miscalculate, however, for Iseut on
her own at court, and therefore no longer suspected by her
husband, has more influence than they have. Beroul refers to

them as 'li troi felon' (4271) to make sure that the audience has got the point. Their association with the evil dwarf taints them. They are given no opportunity to appeal directly to the audience and their claim to be carrying out their feudal duty is shown by Beroul to be a mask for their evil designs, but they are not caricatures. Although they are not individualised very much, they are a potent force, a real threat to the lovers, very convincing in the setting of twelfth century court and family feuds. In the end death is the only solution to the struggle, and it has taken all the courage, resource and luck of the lovers to bring about the death of their enemies rather than to suffer it themselves.

4. Religion and the supernatural

The attitude of Beroul towards religion is hard to assess. The action unfolds in a Christian setting, and the characters are clearly aware of the presence and importance of God, to whom they refer frequently. Many of these references, however, seem to be little more than conventional formulae, exclamations or assertions to add strength to the statement or to express the character's dismay. There seems to be little real feeling in Iseut's cry in the opening lines of the fragment:

> Sire Tristran, por Deu le roi,
> Si grant pechié avez de moi,
> Qui me mandez a itel ore! (5-7)

Calling on God's name here is simply a way of expressing the strength of her feeling. In line 22 Iseut invokes God most forcibly to support the first of her ambiguous statements:

> Mais Dex plevis ma loiauté,
> Qui sor mon cors mete flaele,
> S'onques fors cil qui m'ot pucele
> Out m'amistié encor nul jor! (22-25)

It is crucial that Mark accept the obvious meaning, and so the invocation is even stronger, so strong that it distracts attention from the cunning wording of the rest of the pledge. She is careful not to offend God by telling an outright lie, but her main concern is to convince Mark. Shortly afterwards she again calls on God, this time to add conviction to her denial:

> Ne je, par Deu omnipotent,
> N'ai corage de drüerie
> Qui tort a nule vilanie. (32-34)

Again it is hard to detect any real religious feeling behind these words, just as Tristan's cry to Iseut expresses his emotions but not his religious feeling:

> Dame, por amor Deu, merci! (93)

Many of the references to God can therefore be dismissed as

little more than turns of phrase.

Nevertheless the main characters and the author are very aware of the power and the importance of God. The forces of evil are quite clearly seen to be opposed to God, particularly the dwarf (qui Dex maudie (648)). The barons are described in a similar way:

Un de ces trois que Dex maudie (1656)

Even Godoïne recognises God's power when on the point of death he calls for confession:

Bleciez sui! Dex! confession. (4485)

He is the only one of the three who die who has time to speak at all, and it should be noted that the need for confession when on the point of death is felt to be so strong that one of the wickedest characters in the book conforms, no doubt hoping to make his peace with God. This apart, however, the barons and the dwarf show little interest in or concern for God and His wishes.

The lovers themselves are convinced that God is on their side and that He continually manifests His support for them. This can be explained partly by the idea that God is on the side of the lovers and partly by the fact that the lovers do not see themselves as guilty because the love is not of their choice, at least as long as the potion lasts. Iseut in tears at the hermit's feet denies all responsibility:

'Sire, por Deu omnipotent,
Il ne m'aime pas, ne je lui,
Fors par un herbé dont je bui,
Et il en but; ce fu pechiez.
Por ce nos a li rois chaciez.' (1412-16)

As Ewert suggests, *pechiez* could mean misfortune (*1*, II, 165), in which case Iseut is quite clearly proclaiming herself the victim of chance or fate, and no doubt the innocent victim.

Iseut and Brangien are quite certain that God intervened in the first scene to help the lovers. Iseut attributes to God the inspiration which made her seize the initiative:

Dex me fist parler premeraine. (352)

Brangien is in complete agreement:

'Iseut, ma dame, grant merci

Nos a Dex fait [...]' (371-72)

She spells out the idea that God supports true lovers:

Granz miracles vos a fait Dex,
Il est verais peres et tex
Qu'il n'a cure de faire mal
A ceus qui sont buen et loial. (377-80)

The author in turn strongly suggests that God is on the side of the lovers even when they are discovered. God saved the lovers, who could have been killed:

Molt grant miracle Deus i out,
Qui(e)s garanti, si con li plot. (755-56)

It is certain too that God intervenes to help Tristan escape, although here Tristan is benefiting from the intervention of a third party, the common people, who have risen in dismay at the news of the arrest of the lovers. Because of the pleas of the people God gives Tristan his chance:

Oez, seignors, de Damledé,
Conment il est plains de pité;
Ne vieat pas mort de pecheor;
Receü out le cri, le plor
Que faisoient la povre gent
Por ceus qui eirent a torment. (909-14)

God's motives are clear. He is responding to the intercession of the people and offering pity to a sinner, presumably in the hope that he will repent (Beroul may have in mind Ezekiel XVIII, 23, 32, XXXIII, 11 or II Peter III, 9). Seen in this context, Tristan's leap with the wind catching in his cloak so that it acts as a parachute is, as Beroul says, God showing mercy:

Bele merci Dex li a fait! (960)

This is God the merciful, not God the condoner of adultery.

Tristan has no qualms about using the opportunity for escape. He begs to be allowed his last prayer for mercy (928-32), a request which could hardly have been refused, and is no sooner in the chapel than he leaps behind the altar to the window and escapes. He sees nothing blasphemous or sacriligious in this. Indeed he assures Governal that God has helped him:

Maistre, ja m'a Dex fait merci (979)

Iseut too sees his escape as divine intervention:

> 'Dex,' fait elë, 'en ait bien grez!' (1048)

She can go to her death confident that her enemies will get their just reward (1060-63), a natural if hardly Christian attitude.

After the potion has worn off, Iseut goes to great lengths to make sure that she does not offend God. The whole oath is arranged so that she can tell the exact truth, which will mean one thing to herself, to Tristan and to God and something quite different to everyone else, who will therefore regard her as innocent. There can be no argument that in the whole oath scene she is cynically using the faith of the audience in God's will for her own ends. The concept of ambiguous oaths, as has been shown by Pierre Jonin, was well known in the medieval period, and there were procedures designed to guard against them.[9] Iseut knew perfectly well what she was doing. She could say that she was telling the truth, but she was perfectly aware that her whole purpose was to deceive. It seems hard to avoid the conclusion that although Iseut clearly was in some awe of God, as can be seen from the lengths to which she goes to avoid actually lying to Him, she was not so much in awe of Him that she would hesitate to use Him cynically for her own ends. She comes very close to blasphemy in this scene in her attitude if not in her actions and words. There is no indication by Beroul at this point that he approved of her procedures or that God did, beyond the all-important fact that the oath succeeds. There is no authorial intervention, however, as there was with Tristan's leap. The audience is left to form its own opinion.

The most controversial religious scenes in Beroul are the two visits to the hermit. Hermits, of course, are not unusual in medieval literature, where they have an imporant role to play in calling sinning knights to repentance and interpreting the will of God to them. The first visit seems to fit exactly into this pattern. The lovers find Ogrin 'par aventure' one day, and Beroul skilfully makes the point that they are suffering greatly from the harshness of life in the forest:

> Aspre vie meine[n]t et dure;

[9]See *24*, especially pp.99-108.

> Tant s'entraiment de bone amor,
> L'un por l'autre ne sent dolor. (1364-66)

Their love is so great that they can surmount such difficulties. Ogrin, after warning them of their perilous condition, calls on them to repent. His words are exactly what would be expected. They must confess their faith and their sins. Then God will forgive them:

> 'Par foi! Tristran, qui se repent,
> Deu du pechié li fait pardon,
> Par foi et par confession.' (1378-80)

Tristan is honest with him. They are in love because of the potion and they cannot separate. Ogrin states the position sadly but firmly. They face spiritual death if they do not repent and without repentance there is nothing that he can do for them:

> Ogrins li dist: 'Et quel confort
> Puet on doner a home mort?
> Assez est mort qui longuement
> Gist en pechié, s'il ne repent;
> Doner ne puet nus penitance
> A pecheor sanz repentance.' (1387-92)

In vain he preaches to them (molt les sarmone). Tristan continues to assert his love, and Iseut blames the potion. All that Ogrin can do is to pray for them and to give them shelter:

> 'Diva! cil Dex qui fist le mont,
> Il vos donst voire repentance!' (1418-19)

This first visit has shown Ogrin to be perfectly orthodox and fulfilling exactly the role which would be expected.

The second visit is quite different. Iseut proposes it, as the best course of action if they are now penitent (2270-72). Their motives are at best mixed, quite possibly wholly secular, as they seek his advice:

> Consel nos doroit honorable,
> Par qoi a joie pardurable
> Porron ancore bien venir. (2275-77)

Certainly Tristan sees Ogrin as the means by which they can communicate with the court:

> Encor enuit ou le matin,

> O le consel de maistre Ogrin,
> Manderon a nostre talent
> Par briés sanz autre mandement. (2281-84)

Iseut does envisage going to seek forgiveness of sins:

> Au riche roi celestïen
> Puison andui crïer merci,
> Qu'il ait de nos, Tristran, ami! (2286-88)

At the first sight of them Ogrin reacts as before, calling on them to repent (2299), but Tristan replies that it was their fate to live and love as they did:

> Itel fu nostre destinee (2302)

He wants to bring about a reconciliation between Mark and Iseut (2306), and the lovers are prepared to follow Ogrin's advice to achieve it (2318). Iseut falls at Ogrin's feet begging him to achieve a reconciliation. She does not repent of her love for Tristan (2325-26) but she does pledge that physical relations between them are over:

> De la comune de mon cors
> Et je du suen somes tuit fors. (2329-30)

How far she subsequently honours this pledge is a matter for debate.

Ogrin reacts with joy, as one would expect, at the sight of two penitent sinners. He thanks God for letting him live long enough to see this:

> Ha! Dex, beaus rois omnipotent,
> Graces, par mon buen cuer, vos rent,
> Qui vivre tant m'avez laisiez
> Que ces deux genz de lor pechiez
> A moi en vindrent consel prendre (2333-37)

He promises to give them good advice, but the religious part is dismissed in a few lines, although in these lines Ogrin does annul the sin:

> Qant home et feme font pechié,
> S'anz se sont pris et sont quitié
> Et s'aus vienent a penitance
> Et aient bone repentance,
> Dex lor pardone lor mesfait,

> Tant ne seroit orible et lait. (2345-50)

God forgives them because they are penitent. There is no word of confession which was so important before; there is no imposition of penance. Ogrin moves straight away to the practical means of achieving a reconciliation by lying if necessary:

> Por honte oster et mal covrir
> Doit on un poi par bel mentir. (2353-54)

To achieve a good end, the reconciliation of Mark with the lovers, and to minimise the damage to Mark, Ogrin is prepared to use decidedly dubious means. His attitude to the lovers can be explained by the influence of the school of Abelard, as has been strongly argued by Hunt, who has shown how the innocence of the lovers would be accepted by Ogrin because of their lack of guilty intention.[10] As they had no choice in loving each other because of the effect of the potion, they were not in fact guilty of sin. In this way Ogrin's attitude and behaviour can be explained, and if such an explanation is accepted, it would suggest a date towards the 1160s when Abelard's teaching was still influential. If this argument is rejected, it does become hard to explain the behaviour of Ogrin, who seems to act in a manner most unfitting for a man of God. The most favourable interpretation would be that Ogrin sees Mark as an innocent party who must be spared pain, and so he is prepared to lie for the sake of an innocent third party and to reintegrate the penitent lovers into society. Little attention is paid to the spiritual side of the reconciliation thereafter, as Ogrin and the lovers concentrate on the details of the return of Iseut. Ogrin shows a most unspiritual expertise in bargaining when he goes down to the market at St Michael's Mount to equip Iseut fittingly for her return to court. For a simple man of God his wealth and competence are surprising, but it is possible that he is a hermit who is not in fact a priest, simply a recluse seeking spiritual salvation in his retreat. He could easily be a former knight, which would help to explain his

[10]See *22*, pp.505-11 and 531-34. For a different interpretation see *47* pp.83-85 where Varvaro argues that Ogrin deals with the religious problem in a perfectly orthodox way and is concerned to minimise the social disorder created by the sin which has just been annulled.

knowledge of the court and his worldliness when choosing a horse and a robe for Iseut. As François Rigolot has shown, it is important for Iseut to return in fitting style, and Ogrin is the agent who brings this about (see *42*). He combines the roles of spiritual and worldly advisor.

The organised church has little role to play in this fragment. All its dignitaries are there to see Iseut offer a rich garment in the church of St Samson to celebrate her return:

> Evesque, clerc, moine et abé
> Encontre lié sont tuit issu,
> D'aubes, de chapes revestu (2976-78)

Their presence is part of the ceremonial, and their spiritual contribution is not mentioned. The whole ceremony is part of the ritual of the return of the Queen to society after her exile. The other member of the priesthood who is mentioned is Mark's chaplain. He is important, as he can read the letter sent by Tristan. It seems that Mark is illiterate, as indeed is Tristan who depends on Ogrin to do his reading and writing for him. This is a traditional duty of the chaplain and can be paralleled in several epics such as *Li Quatre Fils Aymon*.

For long stretches of the poem God is mentioned only in conventional turns of phrase which do not indicate any real religious intention. The lovers do call on Him and do see Him as their ally. They trust in His mercy and they are not disappointed. Iseut, however, is prepared to make ruthless use of the faith of others to clear herself, and neither she nor Tristan follow most of the Christian commandments. The one man of God is shown to be very much of this world, cynically ready to argue that the end justifies the means. Beroul's attitude to the guilt of the lovers may well have been strongly influenced by the teaching of Abelard, which was unorthodox where it was not heretical. It is possible, however, that Beroul is reflecting aspects of the outlook of his period, where fear of God was very real, but God was not always in the forefront of people's minds. He was expected to respond to prayers, as He does in Beroul, who shows Him as merciful and pitiful to the lovers, whose intentions are not evil, unlike those of the barons, Nevertheless, this is not a work deeply imbued with religious feeling and, particularly after the potion has worn off and the lovers have made their peace with God thanks to Ogrin, God's role is less significant. He intervenes less and is less respected. He becomes another weapon which Iseut can use.

Belief in the supernatural coexisted with religious belief, but in fact the supernatural as such had a relatively small role to play in Beroul. Certain elements which would now be seen as supernatural were then accepted as normal. For example the potion, which to the modern reader is something alien, would not have seemed very strange to the twelfth century. The audience would know of wise women who could concoct brews for most requirements, and love potions were neither new nor unacceptable. What could be more natural than that a woman as wise and skilled as Iseut's mother was (at least to judge from other versions) would send her daughter away to marry a strange man, until recently their bitter enemy, with a potion which would guarantee their happiness? Three years would presumably be long enough to ensure that bonds of mutual affection would be forged, so that when the potion finally ceased to work, Mark and Iseut would still love each other. This is precisely what happens with the two who actually drink the potion, namely Tristan and Iseut. The confusion of the potion and wine would be quite easy, as 'li vin herbez' (2138) would have been filtered until it was as clear as wine (see *28*). There is nothing in all this that would have been difficult for a medieval audience to accept, particularly when the setting was removed from them in time as it is in Beroul. Beroul's purpose in using the potion is also explicable. For three years the lovers are subject to this overwhelming, irresponsible passion which in spite of themselves controls them. They drank the potion by accident and had had no evil intention, but thereafter they cannot resist their love, whatever the cost to them or anyone else who gets in their way. They are, therefore, as Tristan says, the victims of fate and as such are totally at odds with society, which rejects them, driving them into exile with a price on their head and pursuing them. When the effect of the potion disappears, they are no longer willing to endure any hardship for the sake of their love and are ready to come back into society, where they can continue their affair without overtly offending its norms, at least for the duration of the fragment. By using the potion in the way that he does, Beroul can study the lovers in their clash with society first of all with no control over their behaviour, so that whatever the risk their passion must be satisfied, and while they are aware of their own innocence as the victims of fate; secondly, when there is no potion, much more in control of themselves and now waging war with success against only one section of society. The change of emphasis allows Beroul to make an effective contrast between the two sections of the poem.

Another episode which does suggest that the supernatural was not far away is the jousting at the ford, where Girflet is in no doubt that Tristan in his black armour and Governal are knights from the other world (see also page 49):

> 'Ges connois bien,' Girflet respont,
> 'Noir cheval a et noire enseigne,
> Ce est li Noirs de la Montaigne.
> L'autre connois as armes vaires,
> Qar en cest païs n'en a gaires;
> Il so[n]t faé, gel sai sanz dote.' (4014-19)

Beroul's audience knows, of course, that the two riders are mortal, but to the startled knights of Arthur's and Mark's courts they looked unearthly, and a readiness to believe in such creatures, particularly in a setting slightly removed either in time or space, continues to exist long after Beroul. There is nothing comic or unconvincing about this scene.

Episodes which are referred to in this fragment but which have not survived in Beroul are the scenes with the dragon and the Morholt. The dragon is mentioned in Tristan's letter to Mark:

> Le grant serpent cresté ocis (2560)

Again the medieval reader was willing to believe in dragons in some area or time outside his own. Fighting dragons and giants was very much part of the heroic tradition, and such an episode would seem quite normal in the life of a hero such as Tristan. There are several references to the Morholt, Iseut's uncle, whom Tristan killed when he came to claim the human tribute of the children from Cornwall for Ireland. Whatever the origin of the Morholt, whether he be a Breton sea monster, as the derivation suggested by David Shirt would indicate (see *44*), or a representative of the Fomorians, a mythical Irish race, as Rachel Bromwich argues,[11] there is nothing in Beroul to suggest that he has retained any gigantic or grotesque features. He is the champion of the King of Ireland, the brother of the Queen and a great warrior. His voyage to collect the human tribute reflects several traditions, the Theseus legend, where Theseus frees Attica from the tyranny of Crete, the legends of the battles between the Fomorians and the more recent inhabitants of Ireland, and perhaps the contemporary reality of the raids by Irish slavers on the west coast of Britain. These were mostly descendants of the Norse settlers along the east and south coast of Ireland, and E.M.R. Ditmas has suggested that the duel between Tristan and the Morholt owes more to the Norse style of single combat (holm-gang) than to the feudal.[12] For Beroul, however, neither the dragon nor the Morholt seem to be strongly supernatural. They are awesome and dangerous but not beyond belief.

Although supernatural associations can be suggested for several episodes or characters such as the Morholt or indeed Mark himself with his horse's ears, Beroul minimises the role of the supernatural. There is just enough retained to suggest a different, more colourful world, but not so much that it could force the audience to suspend belief. The supernatural is very much in the background. Beroul clearly prefers to avoid anything that could jar with his picture of society or distract from his main concern, the conflict of the lovers with society. Even the dwarf, who offered some scope for the supernatural, is firmly situated in the court; his gifts are great but no more than a

[11]Rachel Bromwich. 'Some Remarks on the Celtic Sources of *Tristan*', *Transactions of the Honourable Society of Cymmrodorion* (1953), 32-60, especially 39-41.

[12]Article to be published in *Reading Medieval Studies*, 8 (1982).

skilled astrologer might have, and there is nothing incredible about him. ~~rubbish~~

The supernatural and religion are both integrated into the framework of the poem to serve the author's purpose. The supernatural is almost abandoned. Religion has a role to play, but it does not dominate any of the characters. They use it, they think about it when they have to, but for long periods they can ignore it with untroubled consciences, while the representatives of religion are largely ignored both by the author and by the characters.

5. Symbolism

Symbolism in Beroul is not nearly as important as it will be in the *Tristan* of Gottfried von Strassburg, for example, but there are two episodes where the meaning of the author is enriched if it is accepted that he is writing symbolically. I refer to the episodes involving the lepers and to the scene in the forest where Mark leaves proof of his visit for the lovers. These are not the only examples of symbolism, however, as there is the potion, and Rigolot has shown the importance of the visual element in several scenes, the most important for symbolism being the picture of Iseut as she is taken to the stake and the corresponding description of her when she comes to her reconciliation with Mark (see *42*). Beroul takes great pains to establish the richness of the Queen's attire, which Ogrin bought for her:

> Aprés achate ver et gris,
> Dras de soie et [de] porpre bis,
> Escarlates et blanc chainsil,
> Asez plus blanc que flor de lil,
> Et palefroi souef anblant,
> Bien atornez d'or flanboiant.
> Ogrins l'ermite tant achate
> Et tant acroit et tant barate
> Pailes, vairs et gris et hermine
> Que richement vest la roïne. (2735-44)

The purpose is quite clear. Iseut is returning to society as Mark's lawful Queen and she must look the part. Her rich garments and good horse symbolise that she is a lady of the highest rank, fully accepted by society. Similarly, the much shorter description of Iseut on her way to the pyre has a symbolic purpose:

> En un bliaut de paile bis
> Estoit la dame estroit vestue
> Et d'un fil d'or menu cosue;

Si chevel hurtent a ses piez,

D'un filet d'or les ot trechiez. (1146-50)

She is richly but soberly dressed to mark the fact that she is a criminal of high rank going to her death. The dark dress and the loose hair symbolise her disgrace.

Much more overtly symbolic is the role of the lepers. Leprosy was a disease particularly feared in the Middle Ages and indeed long after. It was also held that lepers were afflicted with ungovernable lust and that leprosy itself was a divine punishment for sexual sinners. The punishment suggested for Iseut by Ivain is therefore particularly appropriate. The woman, taken in adultery, will recognise her sin in their company and regret it:[13]

Donc savra bien Yseut la givre

Que malement avra ovré;

Mex voudroit estre arse en un ré. (1214-16)

Iseut would prefer to be burned rather than undergo such an experience (1222). The punishment is physically degrading, socially revolting and symbolically just.

Similarly when Iseut tells Tristan to put on the disguise of the leper when he goes to the ford, he not only puts on a disguise that makes him almost unrecognisable but one which symbolises the fact that he is an adulterer. He himself uses this disguise to taunt Mark, as Saul N. Brody has shown.[14] He tells Mark that he has been a leper for three years, the time he was under the influence of the potion, and that he got his leprosy from his mistress, whose husband was a leper:

Dans rois, ses sires ert meseaus,

O lié faisoie mes joiaus,

Cist maus me prist de la comune (3771-73)

Mark, of course, does not understand, despite the hint dropped by Tristan in comparing his lady with Iseut. Tristan is insulting Mark, making fun of him as a cuckold, but in a sense the joke is on Tristan, as Beroul has made clear the link between leprosy and adultery. Tristan's disguise is symbolic of his adulterous

[13]See *11*, pp.180-82.

[14]Ibid.

passion and suggests very strongly that despite their pledge to the hermit (2329-30) the lovers are as adulterous after the potion has worn off as they were before. Iseut in her oath uses the word 'ladre' three times (4206, 4212, 4213), stressing that it is only Mark and the leper who are involved. Again the symbolic interpretation is clear. Tristan, disguised as a leper, is guilty of lust and adultery. Beroul does not condemn the lovers, with whom he sympathises, but he uses symbolism to make it clear to those in his audience who were capable of understanding it that the lovers were none the less guilty.

Mark's visit to the hut where he finds the lovers asleep, partially dressed and separated by Tristan's sword has provoked considerable controversy, especially over the interpretation of the signs which Mark leaves behind him, a ring, gloves and a sword.[15] Mark has gone to the hut with the express intention of killing the lovers. He is about to do so when he is brought up short:

> Li rois en haut le cop leva
> Iré le fait, si se tresva;
> Ja descendit li cop sor eus;
> Ses oceïst, ce fust grant deus.
> Qant vit qu'ele avoit sa chemise
> Et q'entre eus deus avoit devise,
> La bouche o l'autre n'ert jostee,
> Et qant il vit la nue espee
> Qui entre eus deus les desevrot,
> Vit les braies que Tristran out (1991-2000)

Mark believes what he wants to believe. Credulous and trusting his senses, he accepts the appearance for the reality and decides that the lovers must be innocent after all:

> Bien puis croire, se je ai sens,
> Se il s'amasent folement,
> Ja n'i eüsent vestement,
> Entrë eus deus n'eüst espee,
> Autrement fust cest'asenblee. (2006-10)

[15]See *18*, pp.86-87. This includes the views of *28*. See also *48*, pp.75-104 for a discussion of the whole Morois episode.

The sword between the lovers is a recognised symbol of chastity, so Mark's reaction is understandable, but he has completely misinterpreted the signs, which betray the lovers' weariness and their nervousness rather than anything else. They did not undress completely because they were too tired to do so, and the sword was put between them by Tristan so as to have it ready drawn. Beroul has made it quite clear earlier that the sensuality is there:

> Lor amistié ne fu pas fainte. (1822)

Mark has willingly deceived himself, interpreting symbolically signs which were not meant symbolically.

In the same way the lovers completely misinterpret the signs which Mark left behind. Mark's intentions are quite clear. He wants them to know that he has seen them, understood (as he thinks) and had pity on them:

> Je lor ferai tel demostrance
> Ançois que il s'esvelleront,
> Certainement savoir porront
> Qu'il furent endormi trové
> Et q'en a eü d'eus pité,
> Que je nes vuel noient ocire,
> Ne moi ne gent de mon enpire. (2020-26)

He substitutes the ring which he is wearing for the one on Iseut's finger, shades her face with his gloves, a present from her, and removes Tristan's sword leaving his own between them. When the lovers awake, frightened by Iseut screaming in her sleep after her dream, Tristan immediately seizes the sword left ready for just such an emergency and at once realises that it is not his own. The Queen sees the new ring, and the lovers are terrified:

> Bele, or n'i a fors du fuïr.
> Il nos laissa por nos traïr;
> Seus ert, si est alé por gent,
> Prendre nos quide voirement.
>   Dame fuion nos en vers Gales. (2095-99)

They completely misinterpret Mark's behaviour and explain the situation to Governal:

> Par cest change poon parçoivre,

Mestre, que il nos veut deçoivre (2111-12)

Mark's intentions and the lovers' incomprehension are made clear by Beroul.

What is much less certain is the symbolic significance of these objects and substitutions (see *48*, especially pp.92-93). Superficially, of course, Mark's gestures towards Iseut express his affection for her. The exchange of rings recalls their wedding and thus that he is her husband. The gloves, a present from her, are meant to remind her of the affection which Mark thinks existed between them. The gift of a sword is also an ancient sign of friendship between two men. Mark can reasonably hope therefore that all three signs will be interpreted as gestures of friendship on his part. On a slightly more profound level Mark is reasserting his authority, as argued by Jean Marx. By taking the sword Mark is taking a pledge from Tristan, by giving him a sword he is making him his vassal again. Similarly with the ring Mark is reasserting his authority as a husband over Iseut: '[...] l'anneau est symbole de cette *saisine* qui est un des aspects du mariage [...]' (see *29*, p.294). As for the gloves, which differ from the sword and the ring as there is no exchange, it is a sign both that Mark is reasserting his authority over Iseut, as they too served as a symbol of the feudal link, and of his right to protect her. There are problems with this interpretation. It seems odd that Mark should reassert his authority over Iseut by returning the gloves which she had given him and taking away the wedding ring. These could almost be interpreted as the signs of a renunciation of his authority, a symbolic divorce. Mark's intentions, however, are certainly kindly and Beroul's choice of vocabulary to describe his movements makes this clear; *bonement* (2042), *souef* (2044), *sanz force* (2047), *souef* (2050), everything suggests his care and consideration. It is possible to find more symbolism in a passage than the author ever intended. The complexity of this passage is best summed up by Jean Dufournet. 'Quoi qu'il en soit, le coup de génie de Béroul a été D'UTILISER CE DOUBLE SYMBOLISME pour suggérer le caractère insoluble de la situation et la difficulté constante de communiquer. Il semble bien que ce soit la signification ultime de tout l'épisode [...]' (see *18*, p.86-87).

Iseut's dream is also clearly symbolic of the links between her and the two men who love her. She dreams that she is in a tent where she is attacked by two lions, who despite her pleas for mercy, each take her by the hand. She screams with fright and wakes up to find that Mark's gloves have fallen on her breast (2065-76). It seems clear that the lions are Mark and Tristan who are disputing her, and that the dream is induced by the strain and tension of the fugitive life which the lovers are leading. To wake oneself by one's own screams is a not uncommon experience for dreamers, and it may even be possible for Iseut to have sensed the presence of Mark in her sleep, a familiar smell or noise bringing him to mind although not waking her up. Reality, however, reasserts itself brutally when the gloves fall as she wakes. There seems too little detail in Beroul to take the analysis much further, although a Freudian analysis of the dream has been attempted by Jonin and reviewed critically by Pierre Cézard.[16]

Another possible symbol is the potion itself. It could be the symbol of the overwhelming passion felt by the lovers, the force which makes them cast aside convention, morality and family ties. Beroul does not develop its symbolic side. For him the potion seems to have been something real, the *vin herbé*, the *lovendrant*, which had a limited life and once it had served its purpose would disappear from the poem. Other authors using the legend, who were less happy with the potion, stress its symbolic value, but Beroul does not seem to have been troubled by its presence. He accepted it as part of his story and so, while it clearly has symbolic value, it is much more important as a real drink.

This is true of another possible example of symbolism, Husdent. It is possible to argue that Husdent is the symbol of Tristan himself. He is a danger to society, who cannot be controlled and whom society has to exile if it is to continue to exist undamaged. He follows Tristan's escape route exactly and quickly adapts to life in the forest. He is an exceptional specimen

[16]See *25* and P. Cézard in *Romania* LXXXI (1960), 557.

physically and mentally. The parallel is convincing but the explanation seems over-subtle. Husdent is and remains a dog, which Tristan is prepared to kill in order to save his own life. It is natural that Tristan, a skilled hunter, should have the best dog at the court. As the hound is so devoted, the only way in which he can find his master is by following him, and it is well known that some dogs will accept only one master and are a danger to everyone else. The fidelity of this dog points up the lack of loyalty amongst the humans. There is no need to look for symbolism here. This is an episode which, like the horse's ears, was probably included for its entertainment value and for variety.

There is then some use of symbolism in Beroul, but it is easy to overestimate both its use and its clarity. Beroul's symbolism seems to exist in broad outlines rather than in fine detail, which would explain why it poses so many problems and provides such a happy hunting ground for modern critics.

6. Society

Beroul did not intend to give us a true picture of society but neither was he consciously creating a different world. The adventure which he is describing takes place in another age, that of the past, but it has a precise setting, Cornwall, and his characters are not superhuman. They are the kings and queens and princes of the time coping as best they can with their emotions and the ensuing political complications. Quite incidentally there emerges a very lively picture of the life of his period in one of the more remote parts of the country, although there is no attempt at a detailed picture of Cornish life as such.

Beroul seems to be very familiar with eastern Cornwall. He may have got these details from his source, but as Ewert says, 'it is surely significant that they [the Cornish place names] have been preserved so fully and in general correctly.' (*I*, II, 32) Thus Mark has a residence at Tintagel on the north coast and a palace at Lancien, which is probably Lantyan on the river Fowey. Ogrin goes shopping at the fair at St Michael's Mount. The forest of Morois has been identified with the manor of Moresc near Truro and the Blanche Lande with Blanchelound on the Truro river. Even small details can be shown to be accurate, as in the fact that Iseut has to go uphill to the church of St Samson (see note 3, pp.11).

The accuracy and realism of the geographical setting can be matched by the realism of the political atmosphere. It is not at all unlikely that Iseut as a foreign princess from a country whose relations with Cornwall were bad would not be well received at court. This becomes a certainty if the motives of the barons for pressing for the marriage are taken into account. We do not have the actual scene surviving in Beroul in which Mark is advised to seek a bride, but it is probable that the barons were inspired by jealousy of Tristan and a desire to see him supplanted as Mark's heir:

> . . .creüst pas losengier
> Moi desor lui a esloignier.
> Li fel covert Corneualeis
> Or en sont lié et font gabois.
> Or voi je bien, si con je quit,
> Qu'il ne voudroient que o lui
> Eüst home de son linage;
> Molt m'a pené son mariage. (119-26)

Their fury when they realise that the Queen is, at the very least, favourable to Tristan can be imagined. Iseut would be hated on two counts, her Irish origin and her closeness to Tristan. The court is then split between the two factions, and what we see in Beroul is not just the struggle on the part of the lovers to enjoy their love but also a struggle for power and influence at the court of Mark. The penalty for defeat would be death for the lovers and, as it turns out, it is death for the defeated barons, which helps to explain why the struggle is waged so ruthlessly. The uneasiness of the relations between the principal characters is well illustrated at the end of Tristan's letter where there is a naked threat:

> Ou je m'acorderai a toi,
> Ou g'en merrai la fille au roi
> En Irlandë, ou je la pris;
> Roïnë ert de son païs. (2615-18)

Tristan does not need to spell out the implications of such a threat. As Queen of Ireland with Tristan as her champion Iseut would pose a terrible threat to Cornwall, where there is no-one capable of matching Tristan. Presumably Iseut is her father's heiress, as there is no mention of any brothers or sisters. The Cornish would find themselves reduced to the status they had before Tristan rescued them with no Tristan to take up the challenge on their behalf. The reaction of the barons is immediate and comic in its hastiness:

> [...]'Rois, ta feme pren.' (2625)

They do not want Tristan back, however, and urge the King to agree that he should go to Galloway, another Celtic region, which was very restive under the Scottish yoke and whose ruler would certainly welcome so distinguished a mercenary.

The relationship of Mark with his barons also probably accurately reflects the uneasy atmosphere between the ruler and his men. Mark is very aware that he needs to seek their advice:

> Conseliez m'en, gel vos requier (631)

The barons too are aware that this is their role:

> L'en devroit par droit son seignor
> Consellier;[...] (3112-13)

Nevertheless when his temper is roused, Mark will ignore their advice and drive them from his court. He will accept Arthur's criticism that he listens too readily to others, whose motives are suspect:

> Tu es legier a metre en voie,
> Ne doiz croire parole fause (4144-45)

After the oath Arthur makes it clear that he has asked Mark to mend his ways and Mark promises to do so:

> 'Ge prié le roi vostre seignor,
> Et feelment, molt par amor,
> Que mais felon de vos ne croie.'
> Dist li roi Marc; 'Se gel faisoie
> D'or en avant, si me blasmez.' (4257-61)

The consequences of such a disagreement could be serious for a king, as Mark is well aware. If the baron with whom he has quarrelled is loyal like Dinas, then the result of such a quarrel was likely to be the withdrawal of the baron from the court. Dinas withdraws to Dinan (1133) rather than watch the burning of Iseut but he does not rebel against his king and is soon reconciled with him. When Mark quarrels with the three barons and threatens them with the return of Tristan, they too withdraw from the court, and Beroul makes the threat posed by them quite explicit:

> Cil s'en partent du roi par mal;
> Forz chasteaus ont, bien clos de pal,
> Soiant sor roche, sor haut pui;
> A lor seignor feront ennui,
> Se la chose n'est amendee. (3143-47)

Mark's freedom of action is thus somewhat limited by the power of the barons, who have been able to take advantage of his weakness and his credulity in the past. A strong personality like Arthur gives the impression of being much more in control of his court, so that much would seem to depend on the forcefulness of the individual king. It is noticeable that after Iseut has taken her oath, when Mark is presumably completely confident about her loyalty and reassured about his position, he is in control (4267-68), despite the scheming of the barons:

> Mais, qui q'ait pais, li troi felon
> Sont en esgart de traïson. (4271-72)

The struggle for influence continues even when the King has asserted himself.

The accuracy of the legal procedures used by Beroul has been well established by Pierre Jonin, who shows that Mark follows strict procedure carefully until he hands Iseut over to the lepers, which can be seen as symbolically appropriate.[17] Burning at the stake was not the penalty for adultery, but adultery by the Queen was seen as treason, which could be punished by death at the stake. Dinas's protest that the case requires a formal judgement can be seen as him fulfilling his duties as seneschal, the officer charged with the administration of justice. The procedure for the oath-taking ceremony is also in accord with contemporary practice, given that Iseut had already stipulated that it was to be one of her own devising, a demand which was not irregular, as she had volunteered to take the oath.

There are many revealing glimpses of the society for which Beroul was writing. Tristan bemoans his poverty and the fact that with his armour in pawn he will count for nothing wherever he goes (239-48). Iseut too shows herself well aware of financial reality, with her demand that Tristan should keep whatever he gets as alms and hand them over to her. The near riot by the people on the news of the arrest of Tristan, whom they adore for saving them from the Morholt, and of Iseut, whom they adore

---

[17]See *24*, chapter 2. It might be argued that Mark exceeds his powers as the lovers were not actually caught *in flagrante delicto*. The evidence of their guilt is so overwhelming that no critic supports this (see Varvaro, *47*, p.111). The only point on which Mark can be faulted is in dispensing with a formal judgement as demanded by Dinas (Jonin p.72). His jealous rage has made him lose control, a point emphasised by his giving Iseult to the lepers.

for her beauty, reflects the turbulent townlife of the period, although the Cornish townsmen are not so effective as their continental counterparts in epic poems such as *Li Quatre Fils Aymon*. The presence of the huge audience at the oath-taking ceremony is also convincing. It is an essential part of Iseut's plan to turn it into as public an affair as possible to reduce the chance of Tristan being noticed, and to have as many witnesses as possible there to see her triumph. It is, however, a heaven-sent opportunity for the people to find some entertainment and relaxation. A queen taking a public oath to prove her fidelity was, after all, a sensational and exciting event by any standards and would certainly be a big attraction in an age when entertainment was always in short supply.

The relative informality of Mark's court also rings true. It may be old-fashioned, echoing a previous period, but nevertheless it reflects a way of life when the king was close to his people. Life at court is quite simple, with squires and favourites sleeping in the royal bedchamber. The Queen could have dealt with soiled bedlinen without provoking comment, to judge from Beroul's remark about Iseut changing the sheets:

> Ha! Dex, qel duel que la roïne
> N'avot les dras du lit ostez! (750-51)

The lament for the glory of court life uttered by Tristan and Iseut when the potion wears off in the forest is not entirely reflected in the picture of a rather more simple way of living which Beroul actually describes.

Access to the court is very easy. Not only can Tristan get up to the palace wall at night to throw in the letter to Mark (after all, Tristan is supposed to be an expert and could therefore be expected to elude without too much difficulty the watch which is posted), but the forester is able to go straight into the court and indulge in private conversation with Mark to warn him that he has discovered the lovers. Mark is then able to leave alone in pursuit of them despite the strenuous protests of his court. Mark alleges that he has to go alone to meet a girl who has summoned him (1932-33), but the courtiers do not seem convinced, although in the end they have to allow him to go. Informality had its limits. The forester would be an employee of Mark, one of the hated enforcers of the forest laws, so that the lack of interest in his death at the hands of Governal is easy to understand. There would be few to weep for a man seen as an oppressor. There are several foresters in the poem, and it has been argued that Beroul is guilty of carelessness in that he forecasts the death of a forester at the hands of Perinis (2761-62) but the forester actually dies at the hands of Governal. There can be no doubt that the forester who betrays the sleeping lovers is the one who is killed by Governal, because Beroul says so:

> Governal vit le forestier
> Venir des tre[s] sor un destrier,
> Qui vout Tristran livrer a mort
> En sa forest, ou dormoit fort. (4045-48)

G. Bromiley has recently suggested that we are in fact dealing with two foresters (see *12*). There is the forester who betrays the lovers and who is killed by Governal, and there is the forester whose death at the hands of Perinis is forecast, who is to be identified with the spy who betrays the lovers at the end of the fragment. The interpretation is very tempting and would certainly dispose of one of the contradictions attributed to Beroul. The presence of the forester at the jousting is in itself evidence of the relatively informal and unhierarchical atmosphere at the court, since a forester was unlikely to be of really high birth. Perhaps that is why the foresters are killed by Governal and probably Perinis.

Realism is further increased by the presence of the lepers. Jonin has amply proved that they were very likely to be spectators at such events, and that Beroul is clearly familiar with their living conditions and the symptoms of the disease (see *24*, chapter 3). Ivain and his companions probably come from a leper village near the outskirts of the town where they exist by begging. Their eagerness to be at such an exciting happening as the burning of a queen and their readiness to take revenge on the society which has rejected them are wholly comprehensible.

Unlike Gottfried, Beroul makes no effort to soften the hardships of life in the forest. This is deliberate, of course, as it explains why the lovers reject such a life the moment the power of the potion dies. The life affects them physically and emotionally:

> Molt i out paines et ahans.
> En un leu n'ose remanoir;
> Dont lieve au main ne gist au soir;
> Bien est que li rois le fait querre
> Et que li banz est en sa terre
> Por lui prendre, quil troveroit.
> Molt sont el bois del pain destroit,
> De char vivent, el ne mengüent.
> Qar püent il, se color müent?
> Lor dras ronpent, rains les decirent;
> Longuement par Morrois fuïrent.
> Chascun d'eus soffre paine elgal,
> Qar l'un por l'autre ne sent mal;
> Grant poor a Yseut la gente
> Tristran por lié ne se repente;
> Et a Tristran repoise fort
> Que Yseut a por lui descort,
> Qu'el repente de la folie. (1638-55)

This is the life of hunted fugitives with a price on their heads, literally without the law, for the hue and cry have been raised. Their diet is inadequate, and each has the secret fear that the other may repent of this hard life, which is shown to be justified as soon as the potion has worn off. They live by Tristan's skill as a hunter aided eventually by Husdent. Governal does the cooking while Iseut puts reeds on the floor of the cabins in which they camp. No wonder Beroul calls it a hard life:

> Aspre vie meine[n]t et dure (1364)

Tristan's skill as an archer is invaluable in surviving in this harsh world. It was not admired as a knightly quality in the twelfth century and probably survives from the Celtic origins of the legend. It would probably ring more true in a Celtic area such as Cornwall where traditions of archery might linger. Similarly the account of the training of Husdent seems realistic and would be of interest to a society in which hunting was an important part of life.

Life in the forest and marsh as depicted by Beroul does not lend itself to elegant combat as described by Chrétien de Troyes. Instead, Tristan and his enemies fight a campaign of ambush and assassination. Governal and Tristan lie in wait for their enemies, scalp them, decapitate them and generally dispose of them as quickly and ruthlessly as possible. There is no nonsense about challenges, fair fights, etc. and all the rest of the etiquette of chivalrous combat. This is war to the hilt, and a nasty, dirty business it is shown to be. Even the so-called jousts at the ford when Tristan unhorses Andret and Governal kills the forester are very rough and ready affairs, probably much closer to the reality of contemporary combat than the idealised versions of courtly romance.

Beroul's society is not in fact at all courtly. Beroul certainly knows the language of courtly love. He talks about the 'losengiers' (144 and 464). He uses the term 'fine amor' (2722) although it does not seem to have the technical meaning associated with the vocabulary of the troubadours here, where it means little more than 'true love'. Despite this there is little evidence of the influence of courtly society on Beroul. The lovers are treated very roughly when captured by the barons. Iseut has her hands bound so tightly that they bleed. It seems unlikely that any king influenced by courtly ideas would hand his wife over to the lepers for punishment. There is little of the elegance and ritual associated with courtly life. The relationship between the lovers is not courtly. There is no waiting, no control and they are equal partners, each taking the lead when the circumstances demand it. It is possible to detect a little courtly influence with the introduction of Arthur and his knights, who leap to the defense of Iseut, mainly on the grounds of her outstanding beauty. Both courts are, however, extremely masculine — the only women mentioned are Iseut and Brangien — and in this respect at least are closer to the male-dominated epics than to the courtly romances where the heroines get their chance to occupy the centre of the stage. This lack of interest in the ideas made so popular by the courtly romances would seem to suggest that the date for Beroul is earlier rather than later or else that, as has been suggested, he was writing for a remote society which had not yet caught up with the changing fashion.

7. Technique and art

Beroul uses octosyllabic rhyming couplets for his poem, using his metre with considerable freedom. He frequently practises enjambement, a relatively new technique, which enables him to use the metre for a great variety of emphases and to render dialogue more convincing and natural or to speed up the narrative:

> Li nains defors est; a la lune
> Bien vit josté erent ensenble
> Li dui amant; de joie en trenble (736-38)

The cesura after 'est' draws attention to the position of the dwarf as the spy at the door. 'A la lune' is in a stressed position to explain how the dwarf could see, and the enjambement of 736-37 and 737-38 speeds up the metre as the poet develops the tension, and also reflects the thought of the dwarf as he peers in and distinguishes the two bodies together. 'Li dui amant' is in a very stressed position at the end of the clause and at the beginning of the line followed by a strong cesura, and the importance of 'de joie' is again stressed by its position, announcing the delight of the dwarf at the success of his plan. The next couplet shows how Beroul can use enjambement in dialogue:

> Et dist au roi; 'se nes puez prendre
> Ensenble, va, si me fai pendre.' (739-40)

Again great stress is put on 'ensenble' at the beginning of the line but at the end of its clause, as it is the crucial word. If the lovers are not taken together the whole exercise fails. The broken rhythm of 740 is completely convincing, expressing the dwarf's whispered excitement. Lines 768-770 show how Beroul can use line length thanks to enjambement to express the drama of the scene:

> Vermel en fure[n]t li drap blanc,
> Et sor la flor en pert la trace

> Du saut. Li rois Tristan menace.

Line 768 sets the scene with the two contrasting colour adjectives balancing the construction at the beginning and end of the line. Line 769 gathers momentum with its rapid succession of monosyllables as the rhythm sweeps on into the next line to come to an abrupt halt at 'du saut', suggesting the speed with which the bloodstains are disappearing. The grim, stark reality is brought out by the rest of the line ending with the sinister 'menace'. The simplicity of the unadorned statement is extremely effective in conveying the tension and drama of the scene.

On the other hand Beroul is not the greatest master of rhyme, twice using the same rhyme in consecutive couplets (725-28 and 2703-06), although Ewert comments that this is a feature found in Norman and more particularly in Anglo-Norman (*1*, II, 4), which might explain its presence, if Beroul was writing in England. There are examples of assonance (331-332) and several examples of successive couplets where the same vowel is followed by a different consonant (713-18 -oit; -ois; -oit). He uses identical rhyme several times (193-94 and 1381-82), which was acceptable despite Ewert's rather grudging attitude: '[...] but we cannot be certain that such identical rhymes were not tolerated if "the grammatical or functional implications were different" or that the poet was not "concerned to produce a simple figure of iteration" and motivated by rhetorical considerations. Alternatively, he may have allowed himself the licence of maintaining such imperfections.' (*1*, II, 5). The omissions and lacunae in the manuscript can be attributed to the scribe although some may be the result of the method of composition.

Muret described the manuscript as a *brouillon* (see *2*, p.viii), that is to say not a finished product but a collection of episodes which could be produced for the appropriate audience. For example the episode with Husdent might be narrated when there was a hunting party present. There can be no argument that Beroul's poem does divide very easily into sections which could be told separately, and one of the features of his technique which may reflect the influence of epic and be an archaism, or may reflect the actual conditions in which the poem would be recited, is a constant gathering of the audience's attention. There are several other signs of epic influence, which have already been mentioned, and this particular technique of calling for attention persisted after Beroul and is still to be found in Villehardouin. Beroul signals a new twist to the story with a line such as 'Mais or oiez de Governal' (965) while a new episode may get a much more elaborate introduction:

> Qui veut oïr une aventure,
> Con grant chose a a[n] noreture,
> Si m'escoute un sol petitet! (1437-39)

It is hard to be sure now whether this was simply a formula to begin a new episode or whether it was a real appeal to catch the attention of a noisy, restless audience. The same episode is summed up for the audience with the rather unexpected line:

> Molt sont li chien de grant servise! (1636)

In this way the close of the episode is signalled and the use of a *sententia* provides an elegant conclusion to an episode lacking any real climax. Beroul is not at all averse to inserting his own comments, whether they be near proverbs like the one just quoted or a cry of distress that Tristan is going to leap into the trap set for him by the dwarf:

> Dex! quel pechié! trop ert hardiz! (700)

Beroul uses this means to involve the audience and to make sure that their sympathies are fully engaged on the side of the lovers. The broken rhythm of the line with its two exclamations in the first hemistich brings out the author's distress, while the second hemistich introduces a note of admiration for Tristan's (excessive) courage. Curses are called down on the dwarf with the same object:

> Dehez ait il conme boçuz! (640)

Beroul is a master of dialogue, which he uses frequently. His characters all express themselves at length, and their speeches never flag or lose interest. He is also very good at quickfire exchanges between characters. These occur in the second part of the poem, suggesting that Beroul was trying a new technique at this point, which was particularly appropriate for the rapid exchange of views or information. The dialogue between the spy and the barons is a good example of the rapidity with which the conversation moves and the mastery which Beroul shows in using his metre:

> 'Conment le sez?' 'Je l'ai veü.'
> 'Tristran?' 'Je, voire, et conneü.'
> 'Qant i fu il?' 'Hui main l'i vi.'
> 'Et qui o lui?' 'Cil son ami.'
> 'Ami? Et qui?' 'Dan Governal.'
> 'Ou se sont mis?' 'En haut ostal
> Se deduient.' 'C'est chiés Dinas?'
> 'Et je que sai?' 'Il n'i sont pas
> Sanz son seü!' 'Asez puet estre.' (4295-303)

The breathless atmosphere is vividly created by this technique, a feeling of the excitement of the barons as their spy brings them news of another opportunity to resume the struggle. Beroul's skill with words has already been fully described in discussing the use which Iseut makes of fine distinctions in meaning to exculpate herself (see pp.17-20).

Beroul does not give the impression of having undergone a full rhetorical training. He can use the devices of rhetoric such as chiasmus very effectively: 'Lui ai chacié; or chaz ma feme?' (3067). The contrast between the two tenses brings out clearly the unremitting hostility of the barons to the lovers, while the use of the verb 'chasser' shows that Mark, for the moment, is viewing the struggle from the view-point of the lovers. Poetic instinct may be the explanation for some of the other devices such as *exclamatio* and *interrogatio*: 'Ha! Dex, po[r]qoi ne les ocist?' (825) where these reveal the intensity of the author's emotional involvement in the drama. Beroul, after all, knows how to use contrast very effectively, as in 866: 'Or vient li jor, la nuit s'en vait.' It is very simply done, but the balance of the line and the juxtaposition of the two contrasting nouns serves to draw attention to this very important moment, as with the arrival of dawn the King can give orders for the preparation of the pyre. His activity is stressed by the use of anaphora in the next few lines:

> Li rois conmande espines querre
> Et une fosse faire en terre.
> Li rois, tranchanz de main tenant
> [...] (867-69)

The repetition of 'li rois' serves to stress the central importance of the King. As with the previous example, however, a gifted poet could produce such an effect without having had a full rhetorical training, which may well be the case with Beroul. He does not indulge in the use of many figures of speech, and his adjectives are relatively few and not very colourful. He can, of course, describe a scene vividly when he wishes to, but it is always for a purpose, to concentrate the attention of the audience on the external appearance of Iseut, for example, to symbolise her return to society as a queen, or to draw attention to the success of Tristan in disguising himself as a leper. On the whole Beroul is far more interested in action than in description. As a result his characters are usually doing or saying something which is revealing to the audience and advances the narrative. If critics are right in thinking that Beroul was writing for a rather unsophisticated audience then this is quite understandable. The poet who failed to entertain would not be paid, and the only way to entertain was to keep the audience enthralled and to vary the story frequently. Beroul is extremely good at this. The action is never allowed to flag, but the mood of the poem changes frequently. The tension and drama of the arrest and escape of the lovers are followed by the quieter life in the forest, varied by the near farce of Mark and his horse's ears, the thrill of the faithful animal story, the pathos of the visit to Ogrin, and the satisfaction of the death of the dwarf and an unnamed enemy knight. Then the story can reach a new climax with the visit of Mark to the forest in pursuit of the lovers.

Three further features of Beroul's technique are noteworthy. He has a remarkable skill in creating lines which punctuate or conclude an episode very tellingly. When Tristan has reached the river bank after his leap from the chapel, Beroul comments on his flight:

> N'a corage que il retort,
> Ne puet plus corre que il cort. (963-64)

The couplet is extremely simple and yet it conveys exactly the
desperate state of mind of the fugitive with the desperate haste
brought out by the repetition of the verb in the second line.
Another example of this skill is 3845: 'N'en vit on fors le poil
rebors'. Again the simplicity is very effective, and the picture of
the baron drowning in mud is conveyed vividly to the audience
in the minimum of words. Linked perhaps to this is Beroul's
ability to create in direct speech the impression of the
psychological turmoil of the speaker. This is achieved partly by
placing words in an unusual order, partly for stress and
emphasis, and partly to convey this impression of distress or
excitement:

> Mais Dex plevis ma loiauté,
> Qui sor mon cors mete flaele,
> S'onques fors cil qui m'ot pucele
> Out m'amistié encor nul jor! (22-25)

Iseut's tension is shown by the position of 'sor mon cors',
coming early in the line and the clause as she obviously visualises
the effect on her, followed quickly by the stress on the man who
took her virginity, as she wants to implant this idea in Mark's
mind as forcefully as possible, and the whole sentence ending on
the negative. The unusual, almost incoherent word order both
betrays Iseut's own nervous tension and her determination to
make her point to Mark. The same use of the unexpected word
order can be seen in 2285-88:

> 'Amis Tristran, molt dites bien.
> Au riche roi celestïen
> Puison andui crïer merci,
> Qu'il ait de nos, Tristran, ami!'

The whole phrase 'au riche roi celestïen' is moved up to start the
sentence to emphasise that Iseut's mind is turned for the
moment to making her peace with God. Simplicity and word
order are both used very effectively by Beroul, who is, however,
also quite capable of resorting to the most blatant line-fillers
when he needs a half line to complete his thought or his rhyme.

'[...] ce me senble' (29) or '[...] n'en quier mentir' (64) are obvious examples, but he can resort to more subtle ones, as in the following couplet:

> Certes, oïl, n'i faudra mie,
> Por Deu, le fiz sainte Marie. (147-48)

'Le fiz sainte Marie' is not wholly out of place but neither is it an essential part of the line. This willingness to resort to what are really formulae to complete a line and provide the necessary rhyme is again reminiscent of epic poetry.

Technically Beroul is an uneven poet. It must be admitted that there are poor lines and weak rhymes ('quit' and 'lui' (123-24) or 'feme' and 'reigne' (1115-16)). Even if one accepts, as I do, the explanations of René Ménage for the problem over the three barons or four and the explanation of Bromiley for the deaths of the foresters (see p.52 and p.80), it is still poor craftsmanship on the part of the poet that we should be forced to seek such ingenious explanations. All this, however, strikes only the reader who has time to ponder at length over the text. Even today, when it is being read silently rather than aloud, what strikes the reader is the pace of the narrative, the excitement of the action, the liveliness of the main characters and the variety of mood. These must have seemed even more impressive to an audience whose palate was not as jaded as ours.

8. Conclusion

Beroul wrote one of the great poems of medieval literature. The plot was not his, but he made it his own. His vision of the story is unlike any of the other surviving versions, even that of Eilhart with whom he shares much of his material. His appeal to the modern reader is based on several factors.

Firstly there is his sympathy with his characters. Beroul never hides his involvement with the lovers, and as a result succeeds in involving his audience with them too. They are such vivid, living characters that it is hard to resist their appeal. The spectacle of Iseut, a princess almost alone in a hostile court fighting desperately for her love and her life, and winning at a time when women were not expected to win, is intensely moving. Her courage, her resource and her beauty gain the reader's sympathy, just as they did that of Arthur. Her self-centredness, her liking for money and her vindictiveness make her human and interesting, as she is not too perfect. When Tristan is seen to be so loyal and devoted, but passionate and headstrong as well, the lovers' appeal is irresistible, particularly when they did not initially choose to become lovers. Beroul is too clever to weight the balance too much in their favour. Mark is not a figure of fun, nor is he despicable. Mark too can appeal to the reader, and in this way the full tragedy of the situation can be exploited.

Secondly there is the excitement of the story. Beroul rejects the possibility of analysing the love felt by Tristan and Iseut in great depth. In an action-filled story such as his, such analyses would delay the narrative and destroy the tension. Instead he depicts the effect on a court of such an affair and entwines the political and emotional strands of the story. As a result more is at stake than the personal happiness of the lovers. It is a question of who will have the ear of the King of Cornwall.

Thirdly there is the variety and the richness of the story. Scenes of epic action such as the leap from the chapel are followed by the cruel *fabliau*-type humour of the scene at the ford, where the barons are lured to a mudbath and Mark is cheekily called a cuckold to his face by Tristan without realising it. The suffering of the lovers is not minimised, which means again that the audience is able to understand and feel for them, but nor are the lovers shown to be superhuman. Once the potion has worn off, they yearn for the comforts of court life like everyone else. Court, town and forest are all involved in the story and as the action switches from one setting to another, we learn something of each.

Finally there is Beroul's relative freedom from some of the conventions of his time, by which I mean in particular courtly love. It is very hard for a modern audience to adjust to the artificiality of courtly love, but in a story like Beroul's which is not concerned with such conventions but is instead showing the clash between passion and society, which cannot cope with the effect of such a passion, there is a timelessness which enables the modern reader to participate as fully as his twelfth-century predecessor.

Beroul's poem lives because his characters grip the reader's imagination. We care what happens to them and rejoice with them when Tristan successfully ambushes his enemies. The society in which they live and fight comes to life, helped by the accuracy of the Cornish background. The poem as we have it may be a *brouillon* but there is a unity of characterisation and inspiration which makes it hard to see how it could have been written by anyone except one man who had a clear overall picture of the legend and his treatment of it, even if some points of detail remained blurred. If the majority of critics are correct in assuming that we have about one third of the poem (Jacques Ribard has recently suggested that we may have lost very little: see *41*, p.234), it is a tragedy not so much because the missing parts would probably solve our problems, but because on the evidence we have lost part of a great work of art.

9. The 'Folie de Berne'

The *Folie de Berne* owes its name to the location of the only existing manuscript at Bern, number 354, and the poem is on folios 151v to 156v. It has 574 lines written in Norman dialect and probably dates from the end of the twelfth century.[18] It is traditionally linked with the *Tristan* of Beroul, and its content indicates that the author certainly drew on the same traditions as Beroul, although his interpretation is his own. The *Folie de Berne* has also traditionally been rated inferior to the other surviving *Folie* poem, the *Folie d'Oxford*, but this view is now contested by scholars such as Renée Curtis and Jacqueline Schaefer. As its title suggests, the poem is concerned with an episode in Tristan's career when he feigned madness to gain access to Iseut, and although the author is writing a short poem describing one single episode in Tristan's career, the poem is rich in allusions to other incidents, revealing the author's knowledge of the legend as a whole. The survival of this short poem together with that of the slightly longer *Folie d'Oxford* suggests that this may have been a popular genre: short poems dealing with a single adventure, similar in structure to the *Lais* of Marie de France.

As the title suggests, the poem concentrates very much on Tristan. Iseut does not speak until line 210 and plays a much less prominent role than in Beroul. Tristan is in exile, completely estranged from the court and at a loss to know what to do next:

> Mout est Tristanz mellez a cort,
> Ne sai o aille në ou tort (1-2)

Mark is his bitter enemy and has made public the reasons for the estrangement:

> Clamé s'en est a son barnage,
> Et de la honte et de l'otrage
> Que Tritanz ses niés li a fait. (10-12)

[18]See *51*, p.20, where the dialect is discussed, and p.22, where Hoepffner puts the date between the mid-twelfth century and the early thirteenth.

Only Dinas is still Tristan's friend and warns him of the hatred of Mark (34-39). This warning is the trigger for the action. Tristan, forbidden to return to his country, unhappily married to the wrong Iseut, can think of nothing but how to make contact with Iseut (Mark's wife):

> Ysiaut a il, mais nen a mie
> Cele qui primes fu s'amie.
> Porpense soi qu'il porra faire,
> Com la porra a soi atraire,
> Car n'ose aler en sa contree. (49-53)

His ensuing lament, as Curtis has pointed out, has a courtly tone which is completely lacking in Beroul.[19] Tristan expatiates on his misery and his suffering and his need to see and speak to his beloved:

> Et il [Dex] me doint enor et joie
> Et si me tor en itel voie
> Q'ancore la puisse aviser
> Et li veoir et encontrer!
> Dex! com sui maz et confonduz
> Et en terre mout po cremuz!
> Las! que ferai, quant ne la voi?
> Que por li sui en grant efroi
> Et nuit et jor et tot lo terme:
> Quant ne la voi, a po ne deve. (84-93)

The memory of his victory over the Morholt and how Iseut cured him spurs him into rejecting the cowardly course of not trying to see her again; accepting the need to disguise himself, he resolves to shave his head and go as a madman:

> Por li me ferai rere et tondre,
> S'autrement ne me puis repondre. (108-09)

His actions suggest that the disguise is not inappropriate and that in his desperation he is already well on the way to real madness. The decision once taken he leaves immediately, travelling without pause until he reaches the sea. The author comments that he is indeed mad, confirming the reader's suspicions:

---

[19]See *54* (but Hoepffner dismissed this tone as superficial: see *51*, p.17).

> Et si vos di qu'il a pieça
> Tel poine soferte por li
> Et mout esté fol, je vos di. (123-25)

Only when he has crossed the sea does he adopt his disguise, tearing his clothes, clawing at his face, cutting off his blond hair and taking a club, the weapon and badge of the fool. Driven by his love he wanders through the country, playing his role so convincingly that no-one doubts his insanity. Love inspires him when he reaches the court:

> Haut fu tonduz, lonc ot le col,
> A merveille sambla bien fol,
> Mout s'est mis por amor en grande. (154-56)

The scene with Mark in front of the whole court shows Tristan at his most daring, driven to desperation presumably by the additional torment of being in Iseut's presence. Relying wholly on his disguise as a madman and his reversed name as Tantris he reveals a knowledge of the affair between himself and Iseut which infuriates and terrifies the latter. Powerless to stop him she has to suffer the indignity of exposure at the hands of this apparent lunatic. Tristan reveals so much that even the courtiers begin to wonder:

> Mien escïant, tot avandroit
> Que mes sires cel fol crerroit. (250-51)

Mark, however, wants to go hunting and departs, evidently unconcerned. No doubt the opening of the conversation with Tristan claiming to be the child of a whale and a walrus had convinced him of the man's insanity. The offer to exchange his sister for Iseut, the house in the clouds, the potion, the claim to be Tristan are all seen as part of the outpourings of a demented imagination. Mark is gentle with him:

> Or te repose, Picolet.
> Ce poise me que tant fait as;
> Lai or huimais ester tes gas. (189-91)

Tristan persists with the most daring reference of all, to the discovery of the lovers in their hut by Mark. Perhaps puzzled that the fool should know so much, Mark looks at the Queen. Embarrassed and angry she curses the fool roundly:

> Fol, mal aient li marinel
> Qui ça outre vos amenerent,
> Qant en la mer ne vos giterent! (213-15)

All her pent-up bitterness is expressed in the cruelty of her reply.
Stung no doubt, Tristan replies with a reference to the ring
which she gave him and to his suffering since their separation,
comparing himself favourably to Yder, the lover of Guenevere,
and ending outrageously with the remarks which make the
courtiers uneasy:

> Tant ai erré par mer, par terre
> Que je vos sui venuz requerre.
> Se jë ensin m'en vois do tot,
> Que l'un en l'autre ne vos bot,
> Donc ai je perdue ma joie (242-46)

   Mark's attention is on other things, however, and he goes off
to hunt while the Queen withdraws to her room and Tristan is
alone in the hall, but only for a moment, as the Queen, full of
bitter regret for her love for Tristan, sends Brangien to fetch this
too knowledgeable fool. Brangien's unpleasant greeting is
skilfully rebutted by the fool:

> Si m'aïst Dex, qui vos pandroit,
> Je cuit que bien esploiteroit.
> – Certes, Brangien, ainz feroit mal;
> Plus fol de moi vait a cheval. (276-79)

As Mark has just departed on horseback, Tristan is no doubt
referring to him and his courtiers who have been duped so far by
the disguise. Brangien is so startled that he should know her
name that she becomes suspicious, and observing him narrowly
realises that his physique is not that of a madman, who would
have endured great hardships and probably been physically as
well as mentally deformed. She is not convinced that he is
Tristan although she addresses him as 'Chevaliers, sire' (298),
but his knowledge of the potion convinces her and she falls at his
feet. After all, he is accusing her of being responsible for his
madness, while he believes that the effect of the potion has been
unequal:

> Mon san ai an folor changiee.

> Et vos, Brangien, qui l'aportates,
> Certes malemant esploitates;
> Cil boivre fu fait a envers
> De plusors herbés mout divers.
> Je muir por li, ele nel sant (315-20)

The audience knows from Iseut's speech (265-66) that she is suffering too, but Tristan does not share this knowledge and, self-centred like many lovers, is preoccupied with his own suffering.

At the sight of him Iseut's hatred wells up inside her, but Tristan abandons the extravagant manner of the public audience and behaves respectfully. His suffering is now caused by the fact that his ruse has been too successful. Iseut does not believe him or Brangien. Lonely, frightened and suspicious, she detects a trap, calling him a 'cointe meschin' (371) and refusing to change when he reminds her of Gamarien or even of the time when she tried to kill him (episodes which are not in Beroul as we have him, as they take place either in Ireland or soon after the arrival of Iseut in Cornwall). She cannot accept that his disguise is not the reality. Tristan, however, is happier, because he has realised that she still loves Tristan and this inspires him further:

> Voit lo Tritans, mout li est buen:
> Bien set quë il avra do suen
> S'amor, car plus ne li demande.
> Sovent en a esté en grande. (386-89)

All his references to their shared past serve only to infuriate her, particularly when he mentions Ogrin and asks if he is still alive. Iseut replies with great bitterness:

> De lui ne fait mie a parler!
> Vos nel resanbleroiz oan;
> Il est prodom et vos truanz. (467-69)

Even when she accepts his challenge to produce Husdent, who immediately recognises his long-lost master, Iseut refuses to believe the evidence of her own eyes. Desperately rejecting what seems certain, but which she does not wish to believe, she seeks refuge in the suspicion that he is a wizard:

> Craint quë il soit enchanteor

> O aucun boen bareteor (520-21)

She will not believe that Tristan could cut such a poor figure:

> Tristanz ot povre vesteüre. (522)

Only the appearance of the ring convinces her (540) and the shock is such that she nearly loses her senses:

> [...] a pol ne s'anrage. (542)

Full of regret for her obstinacy she falls fainting into his arms and then turns to the rejoicing Brangien for advice on how to reward Tristan properly, advice which is willingly given and the poem closes on a discreet but sensual note:

> Entre Tritanz soz la cortine;
> Entre ses braz tient la raïne. (573-74)

As Curtis has shrewdly seen and elegantly analysed, there is much here that suggests the influence of courtly ideas (see *54*). Tristan's stress on his suffering, his ability to analyse his predicament, the inspiration which he repeatedly draws from his love, his acceptance of the need to serve his lady and the evidence which he presents of all his past services, his implicit determination to earn the reward which he sees as his due for his service and suffering, and the conclusion itself in which the lady accepts that the reward has been earned and proceeds to grant it, are expressed in terms which are very reminiscent of the language of the troubadours, and are all in conformity with courtly ideas. So is the relationship between the lovers, with Iseut appearing as distant and unattainable until her sudden surrender at the end. The emphasis on the suffering and longing of the man is also reminiscent of the courtly lyric, which, usually written by men, shows far more interest in the suffering of the men than in that of the women. In this respect at least the author of the *Folie de Berne* is clearly very different from Beroul. Elsewhere, however, the style and the language of the author are in the main uncourtly and not without brutality.

He shares with Beroul the ability to set his characters convincingly in their background.[20] Once Tristan decides to act the part of a madman he does it so effectively that all are taken

[20]See *51*, p.16. 'Cette imagination s'accompagne d'une observation exacte de la réalité.'

in by the externals:

> N'i a un sol en la marine
> Qu'il ne croie que ce soit rage,
> Mais ne sevent pas son corage. (133-35)

The details of his appearance and his behaviour are all included so as to carry conviction. As already indicated he succeeds in this daring plan almost too well since he deceives Iseut as much as everyone else, and has the greatest difficulty in convincing her that the madness is an act. The wildness of his opening remarks at the court establishes beyond doubt in the minds of his hearers that he is mad and thereafter he has only to tell the truth, which serves a double purpose. As Jacqueline Schaefer says: 'Because reality is even more insane than apparent insanity, the hero needs but tell the truth' (see *57*, p.8). The truth also reminds Iseut of all that has passed between the lovers. It is intended to reveal to her and to her alone the true identity of the speaker. The technique is a little reminiscent of Beroul, where Iseut was so skilled in the use of words which meant different things to different members of her audience. Here Tristan is not so successful, as Iseut's reaction is not the one for which he had hoped. Trusting only to the evidence of her eyes she cannot accept the madman for her lover, and lacking the detachment and the objectivity of Brangien, she cannot penetrate his disguise. Her mind is too concerned with her fears and suspicions, increased no doubt by the uneasy reaction of the courtiers. Only Mark seems untroubled by the words of the madman.

It is noticeable how far the poem is dominated by Tristan, another feature which does not correspond to the poem of Beroul. Dinas is barely mentioned, Mark and Brangien are very minor characters, each briefly sketched in. Mark, although full of hatred for Tristan, is kind and good-humoured with the fool but not very interested. Brangien, at first ready to take her mistress's part, shows her quick wits in seeing through the disguise and then turns all her talents to securing a reconciliation which she achieves. Even Iseut, haughty, proud and suspicious, is of small importance beside Tristan. We see little of how her mind is working. She says little, probably from fear and shame at the court, and her obstinate refusal to accept the evidence of Tristan's presence makes her seem unsympathetic to the audience, an impression which her eventual surrender does little to improve.

The whole poem, therefore, revolves round Tristan. He is absent for only a few lines, while Brangien and Iseut confer in the latter's room. His love is the mainspring of the action. His feelings of jealousy, loneliness and perhaps betrayal are driving him mad before he ever assumes the disguise. His acting ability, his daring and his devotion carry his bold plan through to a successful conclusion. The climax and the conclusion of the poem are his reward as he and the Queen retire together to bed, with Brangien hoping that Mark will find so much game that he will stay for a week.

The poem has been criticised for being poorly constructed and incoherent, but a careful analysis does not bear this out. To quote Jacqueline Schaefer again: 'Several critics, including Hoepffner, the editor of both manuscripts, had repeated after Bédier that, in contrast with the Oxford text, the Bern *Folie* exhibited the greatest disorder. The observation is in itself correct but this disorder, far from indicating a lack of skill, is perfectly in keeping with the author's interpretation of the theme, a frantic drive on Tristan's part to satisfy one last time his frustrated desire' (see *57*, p.13). The only point which I would query is whether the text *is* so disordered. The construction seems to me logical. Tristan is unhappy in exile and is driven by his love to the point of madness until he decides to return to see his beloved. He adopts the disguise of a fool which will give an entrée to most circles, and acts the part convincingly. His behaviour at court is nicely calculated to achieve a double purpose — to convince the world that he is mad and to alert Iseut to his presence. He is so successful in the first of his aims that he fails in the second, as Iseut too is deceived. Nevertheless her fear and her curiosity drive her to arrange a private interview with him at which he finally does convince her that he is her true lover. Her reaction then is natural and the poem closes with the satisfying of his desire, the accomplishment of his mission. This is a well-thought out, deliberate progression. Despite the wild (but pointed) ramblings in the mad scenes the poet never loses sight of his purpose and of the main action.

There is very little comedy in the poem, at least for the modern reader. The medieval audience might have found the picture of Tristan the great knight hunted and stoned as a madman amusing but it might equally have aroused their pity and sympathy. The dialogue at court is too tense and dangerous after the opening exchange to amuse. Only Tristan's claim to be the child of a whale and a walrus can raise a brief smile, soon forgotten in the drama of his stratagem, as he proves that truth can indeed be stranger than fiction. Mark is too stupid to arouse our sympathy, as he blandly ignores evidence which only Tristan could know, blinded by the disguise of the fool and his own desire to be off to the chase. This is not comic, however, as Mark's hostility is known, and Tristan is so openly courting danger that the audience is kept on tenterhooks as each time his desire drives him to go just a little further to force Iseut to recognise him. There is too much real suffering in this scene and in the scene in Iseut's room for there to be room for comedy.

The unknown author has produced a tense, dramatic poem which reveals fully the suffering and bitterness of a love such as the love of Tristan and Iseut. They enjoy none of the triumphs that we see in Beroul. They earn their brief pleasure with suffering and sorrow. Separation is shown to be warping their minds to such an extent that Tristan has very little need to act the part of the fool, while Iseut is so suspicious and incredulous that she cannot even recognise him beneath his disguise when her own lady-in-waiting succeeds in doing so. The author never loses sight of his purpose and makes impressive use of his short form. He never allows the tension and the atmosphere of pain to weaken. His use of courtly ideas helps him considerably in this respect, as they serve to emphasise the suffering of the lover and bring out his awareness of his unhappy state, and the coarse behaviour of the 'madman' is an effective contrast. The octosyllabic couplet does not hamper the author.[21] He uses it in

[21] Although he can handle his metre (see *51*, p.23 for examples), he is not the

dialogue and in narrative, although enjambement is rare and unlike Beroul, when he breaks a line for dialogue, it is at the regular cesura after the fourth syllable:

'Fox, com a non?' 'G'é non Picous.' (158)

The *Folie de Berne* draws on the same material as Beroul, and the author has the same dramatic talent as Beroul, but they share little else. The *Folie* is much more influenced by courtly ideas than Beroul. It charts the pain and suffering of a doomed love, while he describes the spirited and, for the moment at least, victorious struggles of the lovers to hold their place in society. Beroul shows the interplay of politics and the love affair, but he is not interested in analysing the nature of the love. In the *Folie* the author is interested in analysis but there are no politics. Beroul, on an admittedly much larger canvas, has a gallery of vividly drawn minor characters. In the *Folie* the author's main interest is in Tristan himself.

It is therefore a mistake to try to link the poems too closely. They should be seen as two poems sharing a common tradition but with different interests and points of view. Each is a great work in its own right. Beroul has long been recognised as a master writer but it is only recently that the *Folie de Berne* has been recognised as good of its kind, a vivid, short poem telling of one episode in the hero's career. It deserves to be no longer overshadowed by the *Folie d'Oxford* but appreciated on its own for its own very considerable merits.

most skilled of poets. 'L'art de notre auteur, à première vue, ne s'élève pas à un niveau très haut' (*51*, p.13). Examples are given of his poor rhymes and banal vocabulary.

Appendix

Below are listed themes which appear in both the *Folie de Berne* and the *Folie d'Oxford*. References are given to the Payen edition, as it is more accessible to students, although the Hoepffner editions are still the standard texts and references to them are given in brackets. This appendix was produced with the close collaboration of Dr G.N. Bromiley.

MAIN PARALLELS: STRUCTURE

Berne		Oxford
	The hatred felt for Tristan by Mark	
38-9		161-2
(38-9)		(163-4)
	Tristan's sorrow at loss of Iseut	
47-50		17-24
(47-50)		(17-22)
	Tristan makes for the sea without delay	
120-1		63-4
(118-19)		(63-4)
	The name Tantris	
126-7		315-6
(124-5)		(317-8)
	Tristan disguises himself	
129-38		195-218
(127-36)		(197-220)
	Mark begins to interrogate Tristan	
157-8		267-8
(155-6)		(269-70)
	Madman's mother was a whale	
160		271
(158)		(273)

161-3 (159-61)	*Offer of the madman's sister in exchange for Iseut*	280-2 (282-4)
166-9 (164-7)	*Madman will live with Iseut in house in the sky*	299-308 (301-10)
210-15 (209-13)	*Angry reaction of Iseut*	317-20 (319-22)
252-5 (250-3)	*King leaves for hunt*	531-6 (533-8)
269-70 (267-68)	*Iseut sends Brangien for Tristan*	598-604 (600-606)
332-34 (330-32)	*Brangien brings back Tristan to Iseut's room*	675-6 (677-8)
335-7 (333-35)	*Uncertainty of Iseut*	679-82 (681-4)
344-7 (342-45)	*Tristan complains of Iseut's indifference*	691-4 (693-6)
508-18 (506-16)	*Husdent recognizes Tristan*	899-916 (901-18)
523-7 (521-25)	*Tristan's praise of dog*	931-4 (933-6)
540 (538)	*Production of ring*	957 (959)

Iseut embraces Tristan

552-4   975-6
(550-52)   977-8)

MAIN PARALLELS: SHARED ALLUSIONS TO PAST EVENTS

Berne   Oxford

Tristan plays harp

397-400   351-4, 359-60
(395-97)   (353-6, 361-2)

Curing of wound inflicted by Morholt

401-05   350, 355-8, 361-2
(399-402)   (352, 357-60, 363-4)

Curing of wound received from dragon

406-8   414-26
(404-6)   (416-28)

Tristan's bath when Iseut recognizes the

409-20   *damaged sword*   427-44
(407-18)   (429-46)

Departure from Ireland

426-7   461-4, 624-40
(424-25)   (463-6, 626-42)

Drinking of the love potion

428-38   641-54
(426-36)   (643-56)

The Irish harper incident

380-93   761-74
(378-91)   (763-76)

Mark's discovery of the lovers in the

196-209   *forest*   877-87
(194-207)   (879-90)

Bibliography

Beroul

Editions

1. *The Romance of Tristran by Beroul. A Poem of the Twelfth Century*, edited by A. Ewert (Oxford: Blackwell), Vol. I (1939), Vol. II (1971).
2. Béroul. *Le Roman de Tristan. Poème du XIIe Siècle*, édité par Ernest Muret, 4e édition revue par L.M. Defourques (Paris: Champion, Les Classiques Français du Moyen Age, 12, 1947).

Translations

3. Béroul. *Tristan and Iseult*, translated by Janet H. Caulkins and Guy R. Mermier (Paris: Champion, 1967). This is based on the Muret, Defourques edition and is a careful, line by line rendering.
4. Beroul. *The Romance of Tristan and The Tale of Tristan's Madness*, translated by Alan S. Fedrick (Harmondsworth: Penguin Classics, 1970). A free rendering into English prose.

Critical Works

5. Alison Adams and Timothy D. Hemming. 'La Fin du *Tristan* de Béroul', *Moyen Age*, LXXIX (1973), 449-68.
6. Francis Bar. 'Le Premier Serment ambigu d'Iseut dans le poème de Béroul', *Bulletin bibliographique de la Société Internationale Arthurienne*, XXIX (1977), 181-84. A useful analysis of some important scenes.
7. François-Xavier Baron. 'Visual Presentation in Béroul's *Tristan*', *Modern Language Quarterly*, XXXIII (1972), 99-112.
8. Brian Blakey. 'On the Text of Beroul's *Tristran*', *French Studies*, XXI (1967), 99-103.
9. ——. 'Further Comments on the Text of Beroul's *Tristran*', *French Studies*, XXX (1976), 129-39.
10. ——. 'Truth and Falsehood in the *Tristran* of Beroul' in *History and Structure of French: Essays in the Honour of Professor T.B.W. Reid* (Oxford: Blackwell, 1970), pp.19-29.
11. Saul N. Brody. *The Disease of the Soul: Leprosy in Medieval Literature* (Ithaca and London: Cornell University Press, 1974).
12. Geoffrey N. Bromiley. 'A Note on Beroul's Foresters', *Tristania*, I (1975), 61-73. An ingenious solution to a difficult problem.

13. ——. 'Andret and the Tournament Episode in Beroul's *Tristan*', *Medium Aevum*, XLVI (1977), 181-95. This is another ingenious explanation of a problem in the text.

14. Janet H. Caulkins. 'The Meaning of *péchié* in the *Romance of Tristran* by Beroul', *Romance Notes*, XIII (1971-72), 545-49. An interesting article.

15. ——. 'Le Jeu du surnaturel et du féodal dans le *Tristan* de Beroul' in *Mélanges d'histoire littéraire, de linguistique et de philologie romane offerts à Charles Rostaing* (Liège, 1974), Vol. I, 131-40.

16. Renée L. Curtis. *Tristan Studies* (Munich: Fink, 1969).

17. Edith M.R. Ditmas. 'King Arthur in Beroul's *Tristan*', *Bulletin bibliographique de la Société Internationale Arthurienne*, XXI (1969), 161. A summary of her paper.

18. Jean Dufournet. 'Etude de l'Episode du Roi Marc', *Information Littéraire*, XXVII (1975), 79-87.

19. Jean Frappier. 'La Reine Iseut dans le *Tristan* de Béroul', *Romance Philology*, XXVI (1972-73), 215-28. A subtle interpretation of Iseut.

20. Micheline Hanoset. 'Unité ou dualité du *Tristan* de Béroul', *Moyen Age*, LXVII (1961), 503-33. An answer to Raynaud de Lage.

21. Anthony Holden. 'Note sur la langue de Béroul', *Romania*, LXXXIX (1968), 387-99. An answer to Reid.

22. Tony Hunt. 'Abelardian Ethics and Beroul's *Tristan*', *Romania*, XCVIII (1977), 501-40. Essential reading for the philosophical background.

23. Phyllis Johnson. '*Dolor, dolent* et *soi dolor*: le vocabulaire de la douleur et la conception de l'amour selon Béroul et Thomas', *Romance Philology*, XXVI (1972-73), 546-54.

24. Pierre Jonin. *Les Personnages féminins dans les romans français de Tristan au XIIe siècle: étude des influences contemporaines* (Gap: Ophrys, Publications des Annales de la Faculté des Lettres, Aix-en-Provence, nouvelle série, 22, 1958). One of the basic books for a student. Full of interesting background material, but has more insight into Thomas than Beroul.

25. ——. 'Le Songe d'Iseut dans la forêt du Morois', *Moyen Age*, LXIV (1958), 103-13. A Freudian interpretation of the dream.

26. Pierre le Gentil. 'La Légende de Tristan vue par Béroul et Thomas: Essai d'interpretation', *Romance Philology*, VII (1953-43), 111-29. A useful comparison of the two writers.

27. M. Dominica Legge. 'Place-Names and the Date of Beroul', *Medium Aevum*, XXXVIII (1969), 171-74.

28. Faith Lyons. '*Vin herbé* et *gingembras* dans le roman breton' in *Mélanges de langue et de littérature offerts à Jean Frappier* (Geneva: Droz, Publications romanes et françaises, 112), Vol. II, 689-96.

29. Jean Marx. *Nouvelles recherches sur la littérature arthurienne* (Paris: Klincksieck, 1965).

30. René Ménage. 'L'Atelier Béroul ou Béroul artiste', *Romania*, XCV (1974), 145-98. A wide-ranging and interesting article.

31. Peter S. Noble. 'L'Influence de la courtoisie sur le *Tristan* de Béroul', *Moyen Age*, LXXV (1969), 467-77. Criticises some of Jonin's points.

32. J.C. Payen. 'Ordre moral et subversion politique dans le *Tristan* de Béroul' in *Mélanges Jeanne Lods* (Paris: Collection de l'Ecole Normale Supérieure de Jeunes Filles, 10, 1978) Vol. I, 473-84.

33. Daniel Poirion. 'Le *Tristan* de Béroul: récit, légende et mythe', *Information Littéraire*, XXVI (1974), 199-207. A very useful study.

34. Lucie Polak. '*Tristan* and *Vis and Ramin*', *Romania*, XCV (1974), 216-34. Suggests an Oriental source.

35. Guy Raynaud de Lage. 'Faut-il attribuer à Béroul tout le *Tristan*?', *Moyen Age*, LXIV (1958), 249-70. Argues for two authors.

36. ——. 'Post-scriptum à une étude sur le *Tristan* de Béroul', *Moyen Age*, LXVII (1961), 167-68.

37. ——. 'Faut-il attribuer à Béroul toul le Tristan? (suite et fin)', *Moyen Age*, LXX (1964), 33-38. His answer to Hanoset.

38. ——. 'Du style de Béroul', *Romania*, LXXXV (1964), 518-30.

39. T.B.W. Reid. 'The *Tristan* of Beroul: one author or two?', *Modern Language Review*, LX (1965), 352-58. Supports dual authorship.

40. ——. 'A Further Note on the Language of Beroul', *Romania*, XC (1969), 382-90. A furious response to Holden.

41. Jacques Ribard. 'Un Monde de l'illusion?', *Bulletin bibliographique de la Société Internationale Arthurienne*, XXXI (1979), 229-44. An interesting article.

42. François Rigolot. 'Valeur figurative du vêtement dans le *Tristan* de Béroul', *Cahiers de civilisation médiévale*, X (1967), 447-53. Useful for a study of symbolism.

43. Gertrude Schoepperle. *Tristan and Isolt. A study of the Sources of the Romance* (Frankfurt: Baer; London: Nutt, New York University Ottendorfer Memorial Series of Germanic Monographs, 6-7, 1913, second revised edition 1970). A study of Celtic origins.

44. David J. Shirt. 'A Note on the Etymology of *Le Morholt*', *Tristania*, I (1975), 21-28.

45. Donald Stone, Jnr. 'Realism and the real Béroul', *L'Esprit Créateur*, V (1965), 219-27. Criticises some of Jonin's points.

46. Jean Subrenat. 'Sur le climat social, moral, religieux du *Tristan* de Béroul', *Moyen Age*, LXXXII (1976), 219-61. Very interesting and persuasive, but the conclusions seem a little unlikely.

47. Alberto Varvaro. *Il 'Roman de Tristan' di Béroul* (Turin: Bottega d'Erasmo, Studi de Filologia Moderna dell'Università di Pisa, Nuova Serie, 3, 1963; English translation by J.C. Barnes, Manchester University Press, 1972). An original and important study.

48. Eugène Vinaver. *A la recherche d'une poétique médiévale* (Paris: Nizet, 1970).

49. Gweneth Whitteridge. 'The Date of the *Tristan* of Beroul', *Medium Aevum*, XXVIII (1959), 167-71. Criticises dating based on line 3849.

50. ——. 'The *Tristan* of Beroul' in *Medieval Miscellany presented to Eugène Vinaver*, ed. F. Whitehead et al. (Manchester University Press, 1965), 337-56.

Folie de Berne

Edition

51. *La Folie Tristan de Berne*, publiée avec commentaire par Ernest Hoepffner (Paris: Belles Lettres, Publications de la Faculté des Lettres de l'Université de Strasbourg, Textes d'étude, 3, 1934).

Translations

52. See 4.
53. *Tristan et Yseut. Les Tristan en vers*, édition par J.C. Payen (Paris: Garnier, 1974). Also contains text at the foot of the page. In addition, has texts and translations of Beroul, Thomas, the *Folie d'Oxford* and *Chèvrefeuille*.

Critical Works

54. Renée L. Curtis. 'The Humble and the Cruel Tristan: a New Look at the Two Poems of the *Folie Tristan*', *Tristania*, II (1976), 3-11. Criticises Hoepffner.
55. Krystyna Kasprzyk. 'Fonction et Technique du Souvenir dans la *Folie de Berne*' in *Etudes de langue et de littérature du Moyen Age offertes à Félix Lecoy* (Paris: Champion, 1973), 261-70.
56. M. Dominica Legge. 'Le problème des *Folies* aujourd'hui' in *Mélanges Jeanne Lods* (Paris: Collection de l'Ecole Normale Supérieure de Jeunes Filles, 10, 1978), 371-77. Makes some useful observations.
57. Jacqueline T. Schaefer. 'Tristan's Folly: Feigned or Real?', *Tristania*, III (1977), 4-16. An interesting interpretation.